Believe in the Bold

Custer
and the Gettysburg Campaign

Steve Alexander

with an introduction by Ed Bearss

With thanks to:

- Sandy Alexander
- Lawrence and Nadine Alexander
- Chris Kortlander of Custer Battlefield Museum Garryowen, Montana www.custermuseum.org
- United States National Archives
- UNited Stated Library of Congress
- Gallon Historical Art
- Paul Houser
- Greg Sebring
- Michael Fausell
- Mike Hook
- Roy Kent
- Charmaine Wawrzyniec
- Nick Bauman
- John Hurless
- Chris Kull, Monroe County Historical Museum
- Patricia Stephens and the Norvell Churchill Family
- E. Leroy Van Horne
- Charles Mahoney
- Ron Pickard
- Bill and Jeanne Lyons
- Sherri Schreiner

- Bill Saul
- Rusty Davis
- Val Jonas
- Roger Hoffman
- Dave Ingall
- Ed Bearss
- Robert and Karen Servacek
- Rikki Cloum and Jackie Daffney
- J. D. Jenkins
- Eva O. Shillenburg
- Troy Harman
- Roger and Laurie Harding
- John and Jackie Vohlken and all the Michigan Wolverines
- Brian Pohanka
- Gregory J. W. Urwin
- Father Vince Heier
- Dan Ankney
- Bernie and Nancy McCarthy
- Michael Vallone
- J. David Petruzzi
- Steven Stanley
- David Finney
- Michael Riley
- Maggie Abbott

- Ted Alexander
- Michael and Cindy Wassuta
- Everett and John Horn
- Michael and Mary Goode
- Sergeant Leigh Cole & Kim Bernardo
- Loren Langley
- John Hart
- Jared Frederick www.historymatters.biz
- John Heiser
- Monroe Evening News
- Gettysburg Times
- Bill Schwartz
- Daniel Dunn
- Carl & Trish Moss
- Ernest Lisle Reedstrom
- John Langellier
- Colonel French L. MacLean
- Jim Schoensee , Traverse City, MI
- LaMour Printing of Monroe, Michigan
- Pat Danovich
- Hal Jerpersen www.posix.com/CW
- Don Troiani
- Edwin Forbes
- John Sickles

Editor's Note:

Once again, the author's literary style and-in some cases-even the spelling used in writing this book is a faithful recreation of the way G. A. Custer expressed himself in writing and talking. By retrieving terms, sayings and grammatical constructions in vogue during the late 19th century, Steve Alexander brings the reader to the true essence of the Antebellum and Civil War Period during *"Custer and the Gettysburg Campaign."*

BELIEVE IN THE BOLD
CUSTER AND THE GETTYSBURG CAMPAIGN
Author: Steve Alexander
Text Editor: Kevin Moran
Book Design: José M. López
Front Cover: *'Custer charging at Gettysburg'* by C. Gómez

Published by
ANDREA PRESS
C/ Talleres, 21 - Pol. Ind. de Alpedrete
28430 Alpedrete (Madrid) SPAIN
Tel.: 91 857 00 08 - Fax: 91 857 00 48
www.andreapresspublishing.com
sales@andrea.com

Distributed in USA and Canada by:

ANDREA DEPOT USA, INC.
1822 HOLLY RD., SUITE 110
CORPUS CHRISTI TX 78417
TEXAS - USA
Phone: 361-334-1625
Fax: 361-334-2955
orders@andreadepotusa.com
www.andreadepotusa.com

Distributed in the UE by:

ANDREA EUROPE, S.L.
C/ Talleres, 21 - Pol. Ind. de Alpedrete
28430 Alpedrete (Madrid) Spain
Tel.: (34) 91 857 00 08
Fax: (34) 91 857 00 48
orders@andreaeurope.com
www.andreaeurope.com

Printed in Spain

ISBN: 978-84-96658-43-1
Depósito Legal: M-10629-2013

Dedication

While Everett and John Horn along with Michael and Cindy
Wassuta and Mary Goode make certain this General Custer
is always mounted, it's Jeanne Lyons and the late Joseph
Corrigan, Last of the Horse Mounted Seventh Cavalry, who
nurtured and instilled in me the knowledge, appreciation and
Love of the Horse.
Therefore it is to these people this book is dedicated,
- for without them, - there would only be words on paper.

Steve Alexander

Photo Courtesy of Jim Schoensee, Traverse City, MI

> *"Steve Alexander is the closest thing to George Armstrong Custer, since Custer himself walked the earth." February 9, 2013 testimonial by Colonel French L. MacLean, Author of "Custer's Best: The Story of Company M, 7th Cavalry at the Little Bighorn."*

Actor, Author, Living Historian: Steve Alexander has written, ridden and relived Custer's life from minute details to the monumental moments more than any man who has ever portrayed the Buckskin Cavalier, earning him the title, *"Foremost Custer Living Historian"* proclaimed by the United States Congress and is acknowledged by both the Michigan and Ohio Senates for his lifetime work. He is the author of the 2010 quintessential biography *"G. A. Custer to the Little Big Horn"* and has appeared in more than forty docudramas and films as the General. Most recently the History Channel's *"Custer's Last Man," "Command Decisions," "History Hogs: On The Trail with General Custer"* and *"Little Big Horn – The Untold Story."* Both A&E's Biography of Custer and Bill Kurtis New Explorers *"Betrayal at Little Big Horn,"* received awards for the top historical presentations in 1998 and 99.

Easily recognizable to the people of Nebraska, Kansas and South Dakota, Steve has also portrayed *"The Boy General"* in New Rumley, Ohio (the birth site) and participated in ceremonies at West Point Military Academy. From Colorado to the Canadian Rockies he's traveled by train, steamboat and horseback reliving a past few people experience from the pages of history books. Consulted by universities and historical institutions, and often called upon to speak for the Smithsonian Associates' *"Teaching History"* workshops. Steve was chosen to write the texts of the new historical markers in Tontogany, Ohio and Hunterstown, Pennsylvania annually representing General Custer at Gettysburg, Appomattox and other Civil War events. In 2005 he was honored by and represented the state of North Dakota during the Presidential Inaugural Parade in Washington, D.C. He and his wife Sandy own and reside in the original restored Bacon-Custer home in Monroe, Michigan, the General's adopted hometown.

Instrumental in reestablishing the Annual Custer's Last Stand Reenactment in Hardin, Montana, he now participates in the Real Bird Reenactment of the Little Big Horn on the Original Battlefield each year, during the Anniversary weekend.   Steve is the recipient of the Custer Battlefield Historical and Museum Association's Editor's Choice Award and duly honored by Joe Medicine Crow, Tribal Historian bestowing the Crow Indian name Ika' Dieux' Daka', *"Son of the Morning Star"* a name previously held by only one man, George Armstrong Custer.

Index

Brigadier General G.A. Custer 1863-1864
by C. Gómez

Preamble

It is an honor to introduce a man who has inspired countless Civil War enthusiasts, Edwin Cole Bearss, Historian Emeritus of the National Park Service. He has been called a *"national treasure"* for his incredible knowledge of United States military history, particularly the Civil War, and *"leading the charge"* for battlefield preservation.

It is fitting that Ed would write the introduction for *"The General's"* book about George Armstrong Custer's exploits at Gettysburg, as he grew up near the Little Big Horn Battlefield in Montana. Ed joined the United States Marine Corps during World War II and was severely wounded by Japanese machine gun fire in January 1944, spending numerous months in recovery. He received a Bachelor of Science degree in Foreign Service from Georgetown University in 1949 and a Masters degree in History from Indiana University in 1955.

Ed began his career with the National Park Service in 1955 as the park historian at Vicksburg National Military Park in Mississippi. He was very instrumental in researching and finding the location of the gunboat U.S.S. Cairo and raising it from the bottom of the Yazoo River. Ed's positions with the National Park Service have included: research historian for the Southeast Regional Office, staff historian for the Division of History in Washington D. C., staff historian for the Denver Service Center, chief historian of the National Park Service and special assistant to the director.

He is the author of many articles and books including *Hard Luck Ironclad: The Sinking and Salvage of the Cairo, The Vicksburg Campaign Trilogy and Fields of Honor: Pivotal Battles of the Civil War.* He also has prepared numerous studies for National Park historical sites and is the assistant editor of Gettysburg Magazine.

Ed became nationally known for his commentary on the Ken Burns' PBS series *"The Civil War"* and A & E Network's *"Civil War Journal"*. He has received many honors including the Distinguished Service Award from the Department of the Interior in 1983 and the initial Civil War Preservation Trust's Ed Bearss Award for achievement in historic preservation in 2001.

Today Ed is the foremost Civil War historian and is well known for his extremely popular battlefield tours, more than 200 a year! He advocates walking the actual ground where battles occurred for a clearer understanding of them. His unique presentation style and commanding voice, filled with intriguing antidotes from his astonishing memory, provide *"battlefield trampers"* a transformation back to the 1860's. His participants become so transfixed on each word that they want to hear and see more and more!

David Ingall
Former Assistant Director, Monroe County Historical Museum
Co-Author, Glory, Valor & Sacrifice:
Michigan Sites Significant To The Civil War

Introduction

*"The trumpets are playing, thirteen hundred sabers are drawn.
They flash in the sun.*

The Confederates are coming toward them:

five regiments, riding boot to spur.

Men of Michigan, are you ready? Charrrrrrrge!"[101]

Ed Bearss, National Park Service Chief Historian Emeritus

from a

Cameron Davidson photo in the Smithsonian Magazine

In mid-December 2012, as I was hurrying to catch an airplane for Mississippi to spend Christmas with my daughter and her youngest son, I was surprised to receive a telephone call from Steve Alexander, author and living history extraordinaire. He told me he was working on a manuscript center staging George Armstrong Custer and his role in the Gettysburg Campaign for publication in conjunction with the sesquicentennial. I was not surprised by what Alexander told me, because it was in the closing day of that campaign that as a *"Boy General,"* Custer first distinguished himself as a dashing and brave leader of horse soldiers in combat. Moreover, I knew that Steve would be a natural to meet this challenge as I was familiar with his talents as an historian. But more important was the skill that enables him to capture Custer's mannerisms, gestures and mindset in his assumption of Custer's personality.

In my more than 58 years as an historian and battlefield guide who has led tours of all of American Wars from 1755 through World War II, I have seen few *"Living Historians"* who better combine knowledge of the individual and the events as portrayed by Alexander.   He is in a class in this respect with Jim Getty as President Lincoln and Andy Waskie as Major General George Gordon Meade.

My introduction to Steve Alexander as General Custer came in the final week of June, 1991 at the 115th Anniversary of the Battle of the Little Bighorn. I was then the National Park Service's Chief Historian.

On Sunday on the day in question, I, along with Joe Medicine Crow, were to be principal speakers at a ceremony where the NPS was reburying in the Custer Battlefield National Cemetery the skeletal remains of a 7th Cavalry trooper who had lost his life as Major Marcus Reno's battalion fled through the woods, sought to cross the Little Bighorn, and scale the steep bluffs leading to the Reno-Benteen siege site. Also present was the color guard from the 7th Cavalry to render military honors to their fallen comrade.

Park Superintendent Barbara Booher was present as master of ceremonies. As the first female and Indian in that position, she found herself in a challenging position with many hard line Custer buffs who took umbrage with the pending NPS's decision to redesignate Custer Battlefield National Monument as the Little Bighorn Battlefield National Monument. In addition the same constituents were unhappy with the NPS's increased focus on the Indian perspectives and interpretation of the battle.

Among the guests that day was Steve Alexander highlighting his Custer persona. I stopped and listened as General Custer talked with Ms. Booher in a friendly way and advised her on how to cope with those Custer buffs who were critical of what they saw as changes in how the NPS was managing the Park with a view toward political correctness. I was impressed with what Alexander was saying and for a moment I thought I had stepped back in time and was in the presence of GAC.

I next met Steve Alexander in March, 2008 at the annual Civil War Seminars and Tours sponsored by the Greater Chambersburg Chamber of Commerce. It was good to see and be a fellow participant with Steve, and again he wowed fellow historians and the audience with his first person interpretive program as General Custer.

I spent most of the first 18 years of my life on my grandfather's ranch at the head of Montana's Sarpy Creek. This was 30 miles , as the crow flies, northeast of where GAC and his five troops of the 7th Cavalry met their fate on June 25, 1876. Even so we visited the battlefield on three occasions before I joined the NPS in September 1955. But as all my friends know, I was introduced to the Civil War when I was in the 7th grade. It was then that my father, a World War I veteran, read to me John W. Thomason's *Jeb Stuart.* Stuart, like Custer, made his mark as a dashing cavalry leader. Consequently I became a Civil War aficionado in the ensuing years, reading extensively, particularly during 17 of the 26 months I was hospitalized at the San Diego Naval Hospital recovering from multiple wounds received from machine gun fire at Suicide Creek on New Britain Island on January 2, 1944. Fortunately the San Diego hospital had an excellent library and patients had much free time.

During my 41 NPS years, and especially after my September 30, 1995 retirement, I have continued to immerse myself in leading battlefield tours and keeping current on the ever increasing flood of literature on our nation's military history. As those who follow America's wars know, the two battles/campaigns fought on our soil that draw the most attention are Gettysburg and the Little Bighorn (aka) the Great Sioux War. Consequently, during my

13 years as the NPS Chief Historian, they attracted more attention from my office than any other NPS historic park or sites. It is also of interest to note that Custer is associated with both.   Inadvertently and collectively these two areas generated more letters of how they were managed and interpreted and to whom they belonged to, etc, than any others.

Familiar as I was with Alexander's Custer persona and skill as a Living History interpreter and love of his subject, as hereafter commented upon, I sight unseen accepted his invitation to prepare the Introduction to *"Believe in the Bold: Custer and the Gettysburg Campaign."*   My only condition was that I must read it first. But before doing so, I read *"G.A. Custer to the Little Big Horn,"* published in 2010 by Andrea Press. His latest is vintage Alexander at his best with a large dose of GAC thrown in. This is positive because the author, better than Errol Flynn or other actors who have played Custer on the screen, has lived with Custer for most of his life. I was also impressed with his empathizing Custer's and his command's intimate relationship to the horse, something that too many authors either ignore or gloss over. Perhaps, because of my boyhood and Sarpy background, in my reading of *"Believe in the Bold,"* I immediately noted that Alexander, like Custer, understands and appreciates horses and their role in the Civil War.

Like most ranching youths of my generation, in my years between ten and eighteen, except when going somewhere with my parents I caught, saddled and rode on a horse. First there was Tex, a gentle blazed faced animal, then Walking Brownie an abused horse whose tongue had been badly lacerated by a spade bit by a previous owner; and finally Sparky a tall 22 1/2 hand high black. I rode him until I joined the USMC. All were geldings. Between the 6th and 8th grades, I rode a total of 12 miles going and returning from the one room Sarpy School. Like Custer and his troopers, I had to feed and care for Sparky or face the ire of my father.   I also learned to ride bareback, *"Indian fashion"* and my last ride was on a 40 mile unexpected marathon on a bareback horse.

As an historian who annually, since 1996, has led several tours a year featuring the horsemen in blue and gray in the Gettysburg Campaign that begins with the June 9th Battle of Brandy Station and terminates with the July 14th clash at Falling Waters, I believe I can speak with some authority about *"Believe in the Bold."* Thanks to Steve Alexander, I can now impart to my audience better than heretofore his reason for including these four words in his title.

Foreword

"It maketh leap like the locust; It's majestic snorting terrible.
It paws violently, exults mightily;
It goes to meet the weapons, laughs at fear and is not dismayed,
does not turn from the sword.
Upon it rattle the quiver, flashing spear and javelin.
With fierceness and rage it swallows the ground;
cannot stand still at the sound of the trumpet."[1]

In the face of history, if he was nothing else, George Armstrong Custer was a horseman, a true cavalryman in every sense of the word. In the volumes of study on his desk at Fort Abraham Lincoln, one would readily find works such as, Frank Forester's Horse and Horsemanship of the United States and British Provinces of North America, Youatt's Horse Manual and Nolan's System of Training Cavalry Horses.[2]

From his early childhood to his deliberate lack of study at West Point, guaranteeing him placement in the cavalry, to his vivid self pronouncements and writings on the West, Custer had but one thought, one true calling and one absolute passion and that was the Horse. And it was the horse that would eventually punctuate and define his place in history and romantic legend throughout the ages.

In 1879, James Wilson Alexander MacDonald attempted to capture the essence of the Boy General in his statue, the first rendering and tribute to the fallen hero. Elizabeth *Libbie* Custer, widow of the Golden Cavalier, eventually cried it from its pedestal. Foppish, awkward and dismounted, the monstrosity horrified and insulted the likes of any true cavalryman who ever led a charge in battle.[3]

"General Custer as a cavalry officer," wrote Brigadier General T. F. Rodenbough, *"was in a class by himself."*[4]

"An officer superbly mounted who sat his charger as if 'to manor born.'...Custer was always on horseback."[5]

Confederate General Joseph B. Kershaw remembered him *"...as one of the best Cavalry Officers that this or any other Country ever produced."*[4]

Renowned equestrian sculptor Edward Potter captured that essence on June 4, 1910 when *"Sighting the Enemy"* was unveiled in Monroe, Michigan to universal approval that included President William Howard Taft and the ubiquitous Libbie who pulled a yellow ribbon revealing it to a crowd of 24,000 spectators.

This time the Boy General was mounted on his iron gray steed *"Roanoke."* Interestingly enough, it depicted him in the most pivotal point of his career, *"The Gettysburg Campaign."* Coincidence? You decide.

In my first book, *"G. A. Custer to the Little Big Horn,"* Andrea Press engaged me to write a companion piece for their original 90 mm figurine *"Son of the Morning Star."*

The book was to be a first time read for enthusiasts of history as well as an introduction to the life of George Armstrong Custer. It proved to be a successful endeavor and well exceeded Andrea Press' expectations. Ninety five percent of the reviews were positive and sales for *"G. A. Custer to the Little Big Horn"* outstripped the norm with shelf time well under the usual titles despite the economic times and recent closings of book outlets and competition from new electronic technologies.

The entire tome was researched from my personal library and was produced in less than five months from start to finish.

Although streamlined for a fast read, one of the criticisms was it did not go into depth on particular battles and segments of the Boy General's life that many fans hoped it would. *"Perhaps someday, Steve will write a more in-depth study of this interesting historical character."*[6]

That thought is partially rectified here. With the 150th Anniversary of the Battle of Gettysburg, Andrea Miniatures decided to revisit this amazing story and create the *"Believe in the Bold"* series, devoted to those Bold Knights of the Civil War Battlefields. The premiere figurine places the Velveteen Cavalier once again on the back of *"Roanoke"* in the encounter on East Cavalry Battlefield.

The events leading up to this encounter are diagnosed and analyzed from the saddle if you will from someone who has drawn his sabre and thundered across those same fields of Pennsylvania before sheathing the Toledo Blade with Honor.

Join me once again in a journey through history as we *"Believe in the Bold-Custer and the Gettysburg Campaign."*

11

I

"The War Horse and the Warrior"

"Eohippus" by Charles R. Knight

To know a horse is to know one's self. Cantering across the pastures of your conscience or the frost shrouded meadows of the past, a horse with confidence and agile strength stands with ears thrown forward. A horse's tail transmits a thought and swats at a fly. His nose nuzzles against your breast. It is a matter of trust. You gently place your face against the horse's cheek and breathe into his nostrils. With curry comb and brush, you work his shivering coat and remove the burrs from his mane and tail. In the reflection of a horse's eye, what do you see? Through a prism of the soul, you see the reflection of yourself. To know the horse is to know ourselves.

In the days of dinosaurs a delicate balance existed between hunters and prey in the evolutionary food chain. Catamounts and Camels, Dolphins and Dingoes, once domesticated, would feast at mankind's feed trough. Before they would climb on board Noah's Ark, they had to go through numerous internal and external changes undeniably recognized in relationships between homo sapiens and creatures of the cretaceous/tertiary period. Each species their own unique story. From the beginning, those first amoebas crawling out of the primeval soup, sprouted four legs to stand in tropical savannahs of eastern Europe whinnying for fruit and became Eohippus *The Dawn Horse.*[8]

A herbivore of small stature, that roamed in herds that spent up to 15 to 18 hours each day feeding on herbs, plants, leaves and grasses. Their fragile life expectancy lasted up to 25 years if natural predators could be avoided. Since their gestation period lasted 11 months, mares foaled but once a year, births being normally at night.[11] On wobbly legs they enter the world unsure but determined if necessary to *"go it alone."* Their ability to elude the keen sight of Velociraptor, T-Rex, and numerous Thunder Lizards allowed their survival for a few million years before they evolved into Mesohippus, then Parahippus . As the earth changed so did they, becoming Merychippus, Pliohippus and eventually Equus, the glacial ancestor to the over 150 individual breeds of modern day horse.[7, 8]

During the Cro-Magnon period they were simply known as *"Food."* Even at the dawn of man the horse was a vital element in the human food chain. The meat, milk and hides brought sustenance to early man, but caused a gulf between the horse and his pre-dawn predator lasting several thousand more years. First as prey then as partners, the five thousand year relationship between horses and humans became tenuous and then taming. Domesticated after centuries of being the prey, the equine soon became the constant companion in personality and performance to the nomadic peoples, ancient conquerors and agriculture societies throughout Europe being yet again, reintroduced to the American Continent through the Spanish explorers when Hernán Cortés landed in Mexico in 1519 with a contingent of 16 horses.[8] The Bronze Age glittered in the introduction of the *"Chariot,"* one of history's most important military weapon achievements.[9] For over two thousand years, the horse provided its mobility; and with the new philosophy of *"Transportation,"* the horse moved up the evolutionary ladder becoming more a pet than a pantry pony.

The evolution of the horse by F. Andrea

*Trunk of the Tomb in the "Valley of the Kings",
battle of Tutankhamen against the Asians.
Egyptian Museum, El Cairo*

The Charge by Adolf Schreyer

But when Mars whispered in Hippona's ear, it was all over. From pet to Parthian protagonist, Equus now became the horse of wars. *"The armored Persian horsemen and their death-dealing chariots were invincible,"* wrote Herodotus, *"no man dared face them..."* For the Romans and Greeks, Chariots were a privilege of nobility, not only used in combat but often in sporting events where they might be drawn by a team of up to ten horses. Though they relied heavily on foot soldiers, Romans would walk across countless carcasses before throwing a saddle over the horse's back and learning to ride him astride. Bred for battle, horse breeding became not only a science, but a necessity and pastime that climaxed in the spread of the Roman Empire and need for horse mounted cavalry for all types of terrain. [8]

From the timid Eohippus of Prehistoric epoch to the Assyrian breeds of Biblical times to the Middle Ages, draught horses used to pull heavily laden wagons and plows. Once their numbers multiplied, the hunted now became companions in the hunt and partners in battle. Horses would eat, sleep and die beside the species they loved.   Speed, agility and strength ran in their blood, whether they'd be Mongols on wild Asian ponies racing over the Steppes of Russia or Sheiks astride Arabians crossing a shifting desert. From Visigoths and Knights Templars on large Norman or Friesian steeds[10] to Moors and Muslims whose Andalusian hooves echoed and reverberated on the remains of Roman roads outside Madrid and in Islam proclaimed their horse *"the Supreme blessing."*[8]   While the original Cortés Remuda of wild mustangs proliferated, life for the Nomadic People of the west would never be the same.   All had one thing in common: their bond with man and his senseless sacrifice of their trust and lives in battle. The horse and man had become inseparable, a centaur in myth and an unsurpassed team in reality.

Though we might measure their height (1 hand was the equivalent of 4 inches or 10cm, while the average height of a horse being 15 hands) [11] and weigh the physical organ, it's their spiritual hearts that only a cowboy or cavalryman can comprehend. They say a dog is the Man's best friend, and *"Except possibly for the dog, no animal has contributed more to humanity than the horse. It has fed and sheltered us, and provided us with clothing and transportation; it has been both worshiped as a god and slaughtered to appease the gods."* [18] Few would know and less would understand the relationship between Horse and Man.

Much like the evolution of the horse, the perfecting of a Cavalry Officer occurs over a lifetime. This relationship between Horse and Man often times ambivalent and often overlooked can no more be ignored or minimized or trivialized when a tome is written about the man who was every bit as controversial as was the history of the U. S. Cavalry itself. Tucked in the shadows between the Blue Ridge and babbling brooks of the Dining Fork, lay the lands of the Tuscarawas, the seven ranges, coal country and birthplace of George Armstrong Custer. Armstrong, or as a little boy he was called *Autie* , growing up in the hills of Ohio exposed him to the daily work of the horse and the caring of such prized animals. Although this enthralled him, the beauty of the beast was not truly appreciated in the vast amount of history and changes carried in each step of those four hoofed feet.   From the first ride on a skittish heifer to an uncontrolled flight down Pennsylvania Avenue on Don Juan, he had always desired to be a Horseman. His *"world was filled with challenges that he (could) not ignore...Horses who were dangerous for short legs to bestride must be ridden."*[12]

As a father's love and respect for this valued animal, the boy learned only the love of each of these animals while learning the Farrier trade to bring them surefooted travels in the fields and paddocks. Often seen astride on a little French pony named Platt, Armstrong would ride down to New Market.[19] A cousin, Mary Custer recalled, *"Armstrong was very fond of horses..."*

The Templars fighting The Arabs
Courtesy of "Black Hawk Toy Soldiers"

Autie on horseback by F. Andrea

"The Elected Knight"

"The first tilt they together rode
They put their steeds to test;
The second tilt they together rode,
They proved their manhood best;
The third tilt they together rode,
Neither of them would yield;
The fourth tilt they together rode,
They both fell on the field".[20]

Autie standing on a horse by F. Andrea

Autie at the New Rumley blacksmith shop by F. Andrea

Once he came to see her on horseback without permission and received a severe whipping from his father Emanuel. Later when she came for a visit, Autie demonstrated his horsemanship to her by riding while *" standing up on the horse and running it around in a circle in the barnyard."*[13]   Armstrong's childhood was permeated by the pungent smells of wet horse flesh, the rhythmic clang of hammer on anvil and the rasp of a file on metal; these were the music of his youth.

"It was the (blacksmith)shop that he first associated with the 'horsey-set' of Rumley Township. There, each working day, gathered men with a passionate interest in horses. From them the young Custer acquired his life-long love of the horse."[13]   Treasured memories were the sum of his total life experiences.   Along with Joe Dickerson, young Custer had fantasized about the Knights of Old after Old Foster, their Creal School teacher read Henry Wadsworth Longfellow's *"The Elected Knight"* before the class.

After school they jousted with old Bucephalus and the Cunningham's nag injuring one of the horses and earning Armstrong his Pa's razor strap once again. There wasn't a horse he claimed he couldn't ride in two weeks after his backsides healed. Some said Emanuel was hard on horses. Weren't true. He'd always seen them as tools and not so much as pets. Over the years a blacksmith develops a deep and often times reciprocal love for the equine, this he passed on to his son George.[14] Combined with the patriotism of the 1800's, frontier life, and stories of the founding of this country, the pair of boy and horse grew to value their role in the continued making of history leading up to the American Civil War. Who would have thought this pairing in the early years could have brought a boy to be a much admired General in times of conflict? Who would have thought the animal once wild could carry such a General into history so proudly? For Armstrong, this equine companion brought a calming effect to the stressful life he would lead, always one breath and one heartbeat away from death on the battlefield.[21,22,23,24,25] Custer the man, Custer the warrior and of the Horse for without one there could not be the other. *"The War Horse and the Warrior,"* proclaimed and pontificated in his letters, articles for the Galaxy; Turf, Field and Farm; and in every breath up to the end of his life, George Armstrong Custer was a horseman.

From the stock of Real Horsemen; A later photo of Father Custer on the General's favorite horse "Dandy"

17

18

II

"The Boy General – The Rise of America's Golden Cavalier"

" Come get to the stable, as fast as you're able,
Water your horses and give 'em some corn,
For if you don't do it, the colonel will know it
And then you will rue it, sure 's you're born"[26]

"West Point, New York" by Seth Eastman

Once appointed, Armstrong entered West Point Military Academy in the spring 1857, (of the 108 appointees that took pre-exams only 84 had passed)[15] The Academy, though a noted Military School, was also the best Engineering School in the country. Equal parts math and arts of war; Armstrong had to learn to balance his Pythagorean Theorem with Von Clausewitz and Jomini. He read Napoleon's tactics and aspired to emulate his hero of cavalry, Joachim Murat, and in an age of Chivalry, a generation indoctrinated on Sir Walter Scott and Tales of King Arthur 's Knights of the Round Table,[27] George Armstrong Custer saw his opportunity to excel in Mastering academic equitation. Horses were his passion; at West Point, he would make them his profession. Although Dennis Hart Mahan was professor of mathematics and engineering, he adhered to Napoleon's principles of war and his favorite saying *"celerity"* meaning *"rapidity of action"* was soon adopted by Armstrong.[28] *"The most interesting and exciting of drills whether of infantry cavalry or artillery is the drill at 'Mounted Battery' or as it is sometimes called the Flying Artillery. It is also the most dangerous to those engaged in it, the danger arising, from the upsetting of the gun carriages as well as from being trodden down by the horses who sometimes partake of the excitement to such an extent as to become unmanageable. There is scarcely a season passes by without one or more cadets being seriously hurt and not infrequently killed at these drills. We exercise in Cavalry every afternoon, so that with the various drills together with our studies we have but little time to devote to anything else."*[29]

His cavalry instructor Fitzhugh Lee came from a long line of equestrians-namely Light Horse Harry Lee. And since he couldn't rate number one in his class, perhaps aiming for last might guarantee his spot in the mounted service; *"Who'd ever seen a dead cavalryman?"* Ironically, in the study of cavalry tactics, Custer received poor grades.[16]

While he normally rode a dark bay named Davey Jones,[30] it was just a niche from Sunday in the fall of 1858 on an obstacle course of study-demerits and all- a boy of only 21 would mount a horse named *"Wellington"* and leave a mark everlasting behind a record set by Hiram Ulysses Grant. Nicknamed *"Fanny,"* Armstrong would surely rise above the butt of this joke and foot of his class. That black gelding took to him the moment he threw a Grimsley on his back; Wellington and Autie became inseparable almost besting U. S. Grant's jump on the horse York at six feet two inches. A record at the Academy that still stands to this day.[17]

Flying Artillery practice at West Point

Routine, rhetoric and regulation were interrupted when fiery streaks of crimsons and golds in mercurial arcs traveled across Charleston Bay from Fort Malden, Fort Wagner and the Battery, brought an end to childhood naivety. The innocence of youth wrapped in somber smiles of those who lined the parapets never realizing the effects this light show would have on the million lives over the next decades or centuries to follow.

Hundreds of miles away students in Cadet Gray would read the pages of Harper's Weekly and choose their destiny driven by paper's prose and the lottery of their geographical birth locations. This required each and every student to take an oath of allegiance to the country or resign their commissions. For many this soon to be fought conflict would have a festering resolution in their own determination to *"Believe in the Bold."*

From those halls of academia, Custer would find his position at 1,966 in the long gray line. On June 24, the greatly reduced Class of May 1862 was graduated a year early. Call it *"Custer's Luck"* Armstrong became the *"Immortal"* placing last in standings, but still graduating. It would be almost a month before he was sent on to Washington to receive his orders. Armstrong drew his assignment to Company G 2nd United States Cavalry, one of six original regular regiments in service that would eventually grow to 272 full volunteer regiments the North would muster to combat the 137 Confederate Cavalry regiments that would eventually take the field.[31]

The clopping and scrapping of shod hooves on the cobble streets brought Armstrong to an awareness profound, and by instant sight he recognized it was Wellington that Joseph Fought was leading just outside a Washington Stable, only hours before the First Battle of Bull Run. Riding all night with important dispatches for General McDowell, the

George Armstrong Custer as a cadet at West Point Military Academy

two took to the field of combat with hardly a breather or two. Armstrong sought after and soon purchased this gelding before losing him during the Peninsula Campaign a year later.

Throughout the next few months, he was shuffled from the commands of Hancock to Kearny. Custer's assignments in Virginia saw him on a variety of staffs and virtually participating in every engagement of the Army of the Potomac excepting Fredericksburg and Chancellorsville.

Finally transferred to the Balloon Corps, this honor gave him great consternation yet proved him resourceful and innovative. As one of the country's first *"Aeronauts,"* he suggested rather than a mid-

Graduation photograph Elizabeth of C. Bacon 1862.

day observation that early morning reconnaissance would provide a glimpse when the enemy was starting breakfast fires. His dawn ascensions aboard the hot air balloon, *Intrepid,* garnered him recognition when he observed Confederate forces withdrawing from positions around Yorktown thus relieving the pressure on The Capitol.

Dirty duty on General Barnard's staff followed. When push came to shove, he voluntarily crossed the Chickahominy to observe enemy strength threatening McClellan's forces during the Peninsula Campaign. Barely a year out of West Point, he became a Captain and Aide de Camp on McClellan's staff crediting himself by capturing the first

Confederate battle flag of the Civil War. McClellan would say of him, "simply a reckless, gallant boy, undeterred by fatigue, unconscious of fear; but his head was always clear in danger, and he always brought me clear and intelligible reports of what he saw when under the heaviest fire. I became very attached to him."[32]

I have more confidence in General McClellan than in any man living." Armstrong wrote In a letter to his parents, *"I would forsake everything and follow him to the ends of the earth. I would lay down my life for him...Every officer and private worships him. I would fight anyone who would say a word against him."*[33]

As a Captain on McClellan's Staff he rated a second mount. " *I have captured a secession horse worth at least one hundred and fifty dollars, he is a dark bay. I have him now for my riding horse. I can ride him over a fence five feet high without any trouble."*[19] The Big Bay *"Blooded Horse"* was part of the booty he'd looted along with a Moroccan Saddle, a silver inlaid shot gun and a Toledo Blade 37 inches long, 1 and 1/2 inches wide weighing 2 lbs 8 and three-quarters ounces. Inscribed on the blade in Spanish: *"No me saques sin razón; No me envaines sin honor".* Draw me not without provocation Sheathe me not without Honor. *"...men said that hardly an arm in the service could be found strong enough to wield the blade, save Custer's alone."*[47]

"Blooded Horse" was shot from under Armstrong in one of sixty charges he led during those four years that split our nation. The majority of breeds used during the war came from a vast stock of four- or five- year- old Quarter Horses originating in Virginia and the Carolinas. They ranged from mostly browns, sorrels, chestnuts and light to blooded bays. Lighter grays or whites were reserved for trumpeters and band members. Usually mares or geldings were preferred; some were imported Arabs, Morgans and a stocky Canadian Cob called *"canucks."*

Captain Custer featured here with his prized iron gray thoroughbred Roanoke and General Alfred Pleasonton.

Although Armstrong's choice was the blooded thoroughbred, these horses didn't have the endurance the Quarter Horse or other breeds exhibited on long marches and short of feed.[34] One of them was named *"Roanoke,"* whom he captured and had no intention of riding into battle, *"...because he is too valuable. If he could be got home, he could remain until the war is over."*[19] But fate had another story in store for him.

During the first two years of the war, over 284,000 horses were furnished to the Federal Cavalry. They weighed between 900 to 1,100 lbs and it was hoped they were of good disposition and easy gait. They ate up to 10 lbs of grain each day and could cover some thirty-five miles in eight hours. A walk averaging four miles an hour to a slow trot at six, full trot at eight and full gallop between twelve and sixteen miles per hour.[31,35,36]

A total of over 3.5 million horses and mules went off to war to serve both armies.[48] Inexperience and inadequate training resulted in a tremendous loss of horse flesh. Disease, neglect and war had taken its toll resulting in 1.5 million horses destroyed or killed during the four years of conflict.[37]

A multitude of diseases, injuries and wounds kept veterinarians busy throughout the four years of conflict. Influenza, strangles, digestive disorders, navicular disease and glanders added to the sore backs and general lameness associated with the thousands of horses on the march and in shared proximity that allowed for mass contagiousness. Furnishing horses just water alone was a logistic dilemma faced by the cavalry of both armies.

Throughout the war the Southern cavalry was required to furnish their own horses. Most were superior to the northern breeds and came from progressive American Saddlebred stock and Tennessee Walker Breeds that had a penchant for racing. And as the South was deficient of good roads and primarily agriculturally driven, their cavalry had the advantage. Most Southerners had been raised on horseback and their riding skills came as second nature. Their self esteem was closely woven and tied to their expertise in the saddle. Losing a horse from battle or disease put them on foot and dismounted Confederate Cavalry were regulated to *"Company Q."* This dismounted designation was as much a joke as a necessity, but did not make it any easier adjusting to Infantry for the romantic-minded Confederate Horseman. Inexperienced as they were, many men from the North had signed on to the cavalry branch in hopes they wouldn't have to walk or march. Theirs was a rude awakening when the demands of the horse became all too apparent.

Army request for horses.

Giesboro Point Cavalry Depot. Washington D.C. National Archives.

The First Virginia (Rebel) cavalry at a halt, sketched from nature by Mr. A. R. Waud. Harper's Weekly, September 27, 1862.

Before a soldier would feed himself he must first tend to his horse, feeding, watering and grooming his mount before even enjoying a cup of coffee. After two years in the saddle, the North became more proficient and by attrition there were no more horses left in the South to replace those killed or worn out in service; it was then that the Union Cavalry came into its own.[49, 50] Torrential rains in the fall of '62 brought McClellan's push on Richmond to a halt over the next couple of weeks. The South's premiere cavalier, James Ewell Brown Stuart's first ride around the Army of the Potomac exposed McClellan's vulnerable right flank and attacks on Mechanicsville, Gaines' Mill and Oak Grove ushered in the Seven Days Campaign; Armstrong a constant four days in the saddle, guided brigades and supervised the majority of the removal of the wounded. Although of slight build, but of extreme stamina, he survived on one meal a day consisting of crumbled hardtack in coffee, causing his regimental commander to comment, *"(Custer)can eat and sleep as much as anyone when he has a chance. But he can do without either when*

necessary!"[32] Later Bloody Knife his trusted Arikara scout would claim, *"...no other man could ride all night and never sleep."*[38]

When he did sleep it was short catnaps of fifteen to twenty minutes, often on the ground with the reins of his horse wrapped about his arm. *"Last night I slept on the ground by the roadside, the rain coming down in torrents, our wagons several miles in rear. Nothing to eat since daylight. My only protection was a fine rubber poncho given me by Captain Lyon. For pillow I had a stick laid across two parallel rails. Before I got the rails I slept a little, then woke to find myself in a puddle about two inches deep. Later I slept soundly."*[79, 80]

The undue hardships by the end of the Peninsula Campaign having taxed the Cavalry to a much larger degree compelled McClellan to write General Halleck, *"Exclusive to the cavalry force now engaged in picketing the river, I have not at present over one thousand horses for service. Without more cavalry horses our communications from the moment we march would be at the mercy of the large cavalry force of the enemy."*[37] This reference, was of course, to Stuart's *"Black Horse Cavalry"* the terror of the North. After McClellan's removal from command of the Army of the Potomac in late 1862, Custer was sent home on leave to await further orders. A succession of commanders were marched out of Washington including John Pope whose claim that his headquarters would be in the saddle, drew the comment back, *"He didn't know his headquarters from his hind quarters."*

McClellan's next replacement, Ambrose Burnside proved a flash in the pan. His successor was Joseph Hooker who managed to consolidate the separate cavalry units into a single cavalry corps; these fell under General Stoneman.

General Hooker on Lookout
National Portrait Gallery Washington, D.C.

Early in 1863, Custer received his long awaited orders being appointed to the staff of Alfred Pleasonton who had replaced Stoneman and on May 22, took command of all the Cavalry.[39, 40]

Austere, aloof, sarcastic and a bully were the words sometimes used to describe Alfred Pleasonton. Born in Washington D. C. in 1824, Pleasonton upon age 16 entered West Point Military Academy graduating toward the top of his class in 1844 and assigned to the 2nd U. S. Dragoons during the Mexican War. An undistinguished career, but an ability to exaggerate and ingratiate himself to his superiors provided Pleasonton a promotion to Brigadier General of Volunteers under General McClellan.

He soon garnered the title *"Beau Sabreur"* from his style and natty dress. His jackboots maintained a gleaming shine, his hat always on a rakish angle, and the constant cowhide whip was heard to snap and crack against his jackboots while in stride. His presence was pure sophistication and he never exhibited any difficulty making small talk with either politicians or poor Southern share croppers. Although a lifelong bachelor, his charm, exquisite taste and flair appealed to the fairer sex who were not disinclined to frequent his six course meals and exotic wines served from his elaborate headquarters tent in camp.

General Pleasonton on "Gray Eagle", his dapple grey warhorse.

Jaunty mustaches, gauntlets, straw hats and riding whips replaced the nine foot lances, while sabres were removed from the waist and attached to the side of the saddle. A task master with a heart of gold, Armstrong was to write, *"I do not believe a father could love his son more than Genl. Pleasanton loves me."* In any case he may have had a large influence on George Custer who was also known to carry a riding quirt from that point on.[51]

The spring thaw brought buds to the dogwood trees and strategy of the war was beginning to change for the Union. The objective no longer was a city, such as Richmond, but rather it was to attack and destroy the moving Confederate Army.

The South, only wishing to exercise its constitutional right to secede, had thwarted the industrial might of the North up to this stage in the war. Dixie's noblest soldier, Robert E. Lee, and his army had provided the backbone of the Confederate cause, fighting primarily in Virginia, thought to be, the most important theater of the war.[52]

But now, Robert E. Lee's strategy changed as well. Emboldened by success, encouraged by the futility of McClellan's peninsular campaign and elated by victories at Fredericksburg and Chancellorsville, General Robert E. Lee, with the audacity of a conqueror, prepared for the invasion of the North. He was convinced after two years of fighting on his home soil it was time to go on the offensive and push the war into the North's backyard. At the very least secure food and desperately needed supplies for his starving troops. Shortages had forced him to primarily re- outfit from arms, equipment and even clothing picked up on the battlefield.[86] With an army of eighty thousand men, the pride of a proud and puissant people, he was sweeping north, to dictate terms of peace in Philadelphia or New York. The remorseless tread of his triumphant army struck terror to the heart of the Union.[53] Northern papers had written about the futility and continuation of the war. Large lists of casualties and peace advocates called for an immediate end to the killing and popular sentiment was beginning to swing in that direction. The time was ripe for such a movement north.

In lock step with this plan, Lee moved the bulk of his main Army of Northern Virginia using the Shenandoah Valley as his avenue of approach into Culpeper County.[82] Upon *"Stonewall"* Jackson's death, it was incumbent on Lee to reorganize his army. The First Corps he kept in the capable hands of General James *"Old Pete"* Longstreet whom he dubbed *"my old war horse"*; Second Corps Lee appointed Lieutenant General Richard Ewell and the Third Corps he assigned to Lieutenant General A. P. Hill.[54] The reins of cavalry command he turned over to JEB Stuart, undoubtedly one of the most colorful personages of our American Civil War. Stuart was the noted hero of Southern Cavalry victories and the *"eyes and ears"* of General Robert E. Lee's Confederate Army of Northern Virginia.

With a personal staff of fifteen young officers and a retinue of followers including musicians, foreign military officers and some of the country's finest equestrians, he received notoriety and admiration from north and south of the Mason-Dixon Line.

His humble beginnings in southwestern Virginia were to set the stage of a short but spectacular life. Born February 6, 1833 at *"Laurel Hill,"* the seventh child of Archibald and Elizabeth Stuart, *"Jeb"* grew up with a tendency for frequent fighting. Appointed to West Point Military Academy in June of 1850, he gained the sobriquet *"Beauty"* for his constant grooming and his overtly zealous *"challenge from any Cadet to fight."*

Although his father was a reputed and popular lawyer, Jeb would write a relative, *"had you not rather see your cousin a bold Dragoon than a petty-fogger lawyer?"*

The die was cast and he graduated 13th in his class in July 1854. Commissioned a second lieutenant and assigned duty in Texas pursuing Comanches with the Mounted Rifles, Jeb learned tactics that earned him the title of *"the greatest cavalryman ever foaled in America."*[89]

By 1855, he was assigned to the 1st Cavalry at Jefferson Barracks, St. Louis, Missouri. Arriving bedecked with his famous flowing cinnamon red beard and mustache, Jeb began wooing Flora Cooke, the daughter of Colonel Philip St. George Cooke. The two were wed November 14 and were eventually blessed with three children.

Gen. J.E.B. Stuart's Raid around McClellan. June 1862 by H.A. Ogden.

Content with chasing border ruffians and free-soilers, he dabbled in real estate and invented an improved halter with snaps which he coined *"Stuart's Light Horse Hitch."*

Seeking and securing a patent for his invention, he found himself in Washington D. C. in October 1859. By coincidence, his arrival allowed him to volunteer his services to Colonel Robert E. Lee when news broke that John Brown had captured the armory at Harper's Ferry.

Under a flag of truce, Stuart approached the fire engine house where Brown's Raiders had barricaded themselves and demanded their immediate surrender. Several deals were proposed and rejected by Jeb before his signal brought U. S. Marines storming the citadel and ending Brown's reign of terror.

By age 29, Lieutenant Jeb Stuart commanded the First Virginia Cavalry. This unit became part of the famous Army of the Shenandoah, numbering some 9,000 men under the firm leadership of General Joseph E. Johnston.

"Stuart is like a yellow jacket," wrote General Johnston, *"you brush him off and he flies right back on."* Johnston's recommendations to Richmond, *"If you add a real brigade of Cavalry to this Army, you can find no better brigadier general to command it."* Stuart became that brigadier on September 24, 1861.

Although inordinately fond of the ladies, Stuart was a paragon of faithfulness. He never swore, never drank anything stronger than lemonade and religiously prayed. Considered a very sensitive man, he loved to laugh and frequently joined into song with Sam Sweeney, his skilled banjo player and a Mulatto black servant who kept rhythm with bones and entertained all with fancy gyrations.

His usual troupe made up of fiddlers, a ventriloquist, a giant and a lady aide-de-camp also included a Prussian nobleman, Heros Von Brocke, who wrote of Stuart's encounters with the weaker sex. *"Riding up the main street of the village, I was brought to a halt by a group of pretty young girls, who were carrying refreshments to the soldiers."* Upon spying the dashing Stuart, they began to press around him, *"eager to catch the words that fell from his lips, many with tears in their eyes kissing the skirt of his uniform coat or gloves upon his hand. This was too much for the gallantry of our leader, who smilingly said to his admirers, 'Ladies, your kisses would be more acceptable to me if given upon the cheek!'"*

And, oh, what a hero he was! The second year of the *"War of Aggression"* found him making the famous ride around McClellan's Army on the Chickahominy. General Lee cautioned him to *"save and cherish"* the horses and men, but his impetuousness inspired his troops and gained him praise and prestige. Lee's instructions were to gather intelligence, grain, cattle, and to destroy the Union wagon trains operating near Piping Tree Road. To this, Stuart added the capture of 165 prisoners and 260 horses and mules.

The *"Flower of Cavaliers was clad in an old blue undress coat of the United States Army,"* wrote his brother-in-law John Rogers Cooke, *"brown velveteen pantaloons worn white by rubbing against the saddle, high cavalry boots with small brass spurs, a gray waist coat, and carelessly tied cravat. At his side lay a Zouave cap, covered with a white Havelock and beside this two huge leather gauntlets...the figure was that of a man every inch a soldier."*

To impress and reinvigorate the men, Stuart arranged for two *"Grand Reviews."* Each time, Jeb, mounted on his horse *"Virginia,"* rode to a knoll and at the sound of salute, his artilleryman Major Beckham cut loose with 24 cannon. The troops rode by with sabres drawn giving the rebel yell. A second review took place on June 8th when General Lee arrived in Culpepper prompting the critics to complain *"all Stuart was doing was feeding his ego and exhausting the horses."*[41]

When Union scouts started reporting Confederate Cavalry activity around Culpepper County, Union Brigadier General John Buford informed the new commander of the Army of the Potomac, General Joseph Hooker, *"Stuart...is going to make a raid."*[34]

Lincoln, being informed of the situation, shot back to Hooker, *"If the head of Lee's army is at Martinsburg and the tail of it...between Fredericksburg and Chancellorsville, the animal must be very slim somewhere. Could you not break him?"*[88]

Battle of Brandy Station map. Courtesy of Hal Jespersen.
www.posix.com/CW

29

Hooker immediately sent the Cavalry Corps under Pleasonton toward Culpepper in a move across the chess board of the eastern theatre. Organized into two wings Buford on the right and the left wing under the command of General David M. Gregg would eventually challenge the flowers of the Confederacy under Generals Stuart, Rooney Lee, Wade Hampton, Beverly Robertson, Thomas Munford and William E. "Grumble" Jones.[42]

"*I will wake the Gen'l at 2 A. M.,* " Armstrong penned to his Sister, Ann, by the candle light in his tent, "*and at 4 we cross the Rappahannock to strike at Culpepper. I am in excellent health & spirits-am feeling fit as a fiddle-and never felt better in my life, but the chance of being killed to-morrow is just as great as ever before. In case anything happens to me, my trunk is to go to you. Burn all my letters.*"[77, 80] Utilizing the two fords that crossed the Rappahannock, Pleasonton sent the 2nd and 3rd Divisions along with a brigade of Infantry across at Kelly's Ford. Custer rode with the 1st Cavalry Division and a brigade of Infantry that would cross at Beverly's Ford. Arriving near Brandy Station just before daylight on June 9, Pleasonton caught Stuart's forces completely by surprise. Shouts of "*To Horse!*" broke the Confederate calmness at Stuart's Fleetwood Hill Headquarters. "*Yankees! Great God, millions of 'em!*" was heard as Armstrong broke through their pickets riding with Col. Benjamin F. Davis' 8th New York Cavalry.[37, 77, 89] Unable to fully dress, many of the Confederate troopers rode bareback into battle. Davis who was described as liking, "*to fight rebels as well as he liked to eat,*"[78] took a bullet to the forehead and command fell to Armstrong who rode in front of three Union regiments forming them up for a charge.

Shouting, "*Come on boys, Charge!*" Custer led the 8th New York, 8th Illinois and 3rd Indiana in slashing, hacking and chopping their way through. Captain James Franklin Hart of the Confederate Artillery exclaimed, "*The whole plateau east of the hill and beyond the railroad was covered with Federal cavalry. Hampton, diverging toward his left, passed the eastern terminus of the ridge, and, crossing the railroad, struck the enemy in column just beyond it. This charge was as gallantly made and gallantly met as any...ever witnessed. Taking into consideration the number of men(being nearly a brigade on each side) it was by far the most important hand-to-hand contest between the cavalry of the two armies. As the blue and gray riders mixed in the smoke and dust of that eventful charge, minutes seemed to elapse...At last the mixed and disorganized mass began to recede, and we saw the field was won to the Confederates.*"[89] In the melee Robert E. Lee's son, W. H. F. "Rooney" Lee, was seriously wounded[86] and Autie took a nasty spill when his horse failed to clear a stonewall.[78] By evening Armstrong had had two horses shot from under him.[87]

For 13 hours men on horseback and up to 3,000 on foot clashed in what proved to be "*largest cavalry engagement ever fought in the Western Hemisphere.*"[43] By late afternoon Stuart was slowly beginning to get the upper hand. Buford's attempt to dislodge the artillery had not succeeded until Gregg's cavalry division arrived on the scene and the Rebels began withdrawing from the field. Word shortly arrived that several trains loaded with a division of Confederate Infantry under Robert Rodes had pulled into Brandy Station and Pleasonton himself withdrew satisfied his mission had been accomplished.[44]

General John Buford seated with his staff, from left to right: Captain Myles Keogh, who would later serve with Custer in the 7th Cavalry out west after the war, Buford, P. Penn Gaskell, Craig Wadsworth and Albert P. Morrow
Photo from the Library of Congress

Armstrong was later cited in Pleasonton's report of battle and personally permitted to deliver the captured Twelfth Virginia Cavalry's battle flag to Hooker's Headquarters.[78] The contest pitted 10,000 sabres on each side against one another in what was described as the largest horse mounted battle of the Civil War. An estimated 18,000 horses were involved[18] marking the first time success of Federal Mounted Troops against their Confederate Mounted Counterparts with a total of 1,441 casualties.[43]

On June 16, Governor Curtin of Pennsylvania issued a proclamation announcing the invasion of his State.[90] Although the head of Lee's army had penetrated the *"Keystone State,"* the tail remained in Virginia and Pleasonton was not about to let go, at least not without a good fight. The next day the extreme advance of the Confederate cavalry hoping to squeeze through Snicker's Gap, the short cut into Maryland and Pennsylvania was set upon by Gregg's Division at a place in the Virginia Piedmont Country called Aldie.[87]

31

Kilpatrick's Brigade ran into the enemy's pickets just outside of town and drove them unrelentlessly toward Middleburg and Ashby's Gap before the Confederates retaliated with an artillery bombardment bringing Kilpatrick's momentum to a standstill. Armstrong, mounted on his black horse *"Harry"* named for his nephew Harry Armstrong Reed, Ann's son, plunged into a stream to water his steed, then moved downstream toward the rest of the column. As he spurred Harry up the bank, the animal fell over backwards tumbling both horse and rider back into the creek. When he emerged one of Gregg's staff remarked about how the dust had settled, *"...on his wet clothes and wet hair, Custer was an object that one can better imagine than I can describe."*[78] While Kilpatrick's Brigade was largely composed of raw recruits *"Kill-Cavalry"* and Colonel Calvin Douty of the 1st Maine had *"Seen the Elephant"* and were not adverse to take advantage of the rock strewn open field forming the 1st Maine, 6th Ohio, 1st Massachusetts, 2nd and 4th New York front into line to make a textbook charge. As a small boy, Custer had been raised in the hills of southeastern Ohio. His father was a blacksmith and relied on the young boy's knowledge and help with horses. This early upbringing proved an advantage when the motion of mounted fury thundered across the sweeping countryside and Custer found himself once again in front of the attacking column. Moments later Kilpatrick's shrill voice pierced the hot Virginia environ and the Union Juggernaut built to a crescendo of motion. A Confederate bullet found its mark in Douty knocking him from his horse. So too did bullets bring down Kilpatrick's sorrel *"Beppo"*[92] pinning him prone and unable to continue the charge, which was now picked up by Custer, who waving his Toledo Blade, shouted at the top of his lungs, *"Come on, Boys!"* The animated animal and Aide-de-Camp now several horse lengths ahead of the column broke through the southern line and slashing with sabre suddenly found himself on the backside of enemy lines separated from his Union compatriots. If not for the battered straw plantation hat, oversized boots and unkempt curls all carefully coated with *"Dixie Dust"* he might well have found himself a casualty instead of a curiosity as the rebels thought him one of their own. What may have been a crushing defeat was hailed as a rousing success as *"Custer's Luck"* turned an early joke into a life saving disguise and earned him a star. In the galaxy of generals, only a few would stand out like the rising Morning Star of Venus. At age 23 he became the youngest Brigadier in the Union Army. *"I know that*

Charge of General Buford's cavalry upon the enemy near Beverly Ford on the Rappahannock. Harper's Weekly image courtesy of Applewood Books.

you have heard of my good fortune and promotion to a Brigadier General. I have certainly great cause to rejoice. I am the youngest General in the U. S Army by over two years, which of itself is something to be proud of. My appointment dates from the 29th day of June. My Brigade is composed entirely of Michigan troops except my artillery which belongs to the regular army."[19]

The engagement at Aldie on the 17th had importance for Pleasonton and the Army of the Potomac, by driving Tom Munford back and occupying the gap in the Bull Run Mountains where they gained possession of Loudoun County northwest of Washington, just under Frederick, Maryland, and so pushed the Confederate advance farther to the west than had been its best route. Secondly it drove Stuart 's cavalry back toward the main column in the Shenandoah Valley striking him both at Middleburg and Upperville. The union lost 613 men at Aldie, Middleburg and Upperville compared to the 510 Confederate casualties but accomplished the main objective of throwing Stuart back into the valley.[85] For Armstrong Custer it brought responsibilities, but not difficulties for those who served with him to *Believe in the Bold!*

George Armstrong Custer Battles J.E.B. Stuart's Cavalry at the Battle of Aldie June 17, 1863

By James Holloway from the Collection of John Danovich

Custer at Aldie

"On the Road to Gettysburg"

III

"Drums and trumpets echo loudly,
Wave the crimson banners proudly,
From balcony the King looked on,
In the play of spears,
Fell all the cavaliers,
Before the monarch's stalwart son"[45]

"It was raining, muddy. I'd had no lunch or dinner. I came back to the orderly tent late at night, and my fellow staff officers greeted me: 'Here's the General,' they said. 'Here, give General Custer a chair.' 'How's the General feeling this evening?' And so on. I had made the mistake of speaking to them of my ambitions. But I was in no mood for teasing that night, and I made some sharp reply, and would have gone on. But then George Yates—dear old George Yates, who never went in for that sort of thing— said, 'Look on the desk, Custer. Look on the desk.'

"And there, on the desk , was a big fat envelope, a War Department envelope, addressed to 'Brigadier General George Armstrong Custer.' General Custer"[93]

That is how Robert Ingham describes the promotion in his play *"Custer."* A very similar scenario was enacted by Errol Flynn in *"They Died With Their Boots On."* But after years of research and groundbreaking investigation, Robert Servacek solved the case with *"Custer His Promotion in Frederick, Maryland."*

In the early morning hours of Sunday, June 28th, George Gordon Meade awoke on the outskirts of Frederick , Maryland to the news he was now Commander of the Army of the Potomac. Assembling his officers, he, in essence, asked what they needed to get the job done. Pleasonton politically maneuvered to get most of the foreigners off his staff and replaced them with new blood, specifically the promotion to Brigadier General of three men in their twenties, Wesley Merritt, Elon Farnsworth and George Armstrong Custer.[94]

Armstrong had been out all evening checking pickets and vedettes in the driving downpour and clinging mud,[95] as was his usual, accompanied by Joseph Fought, the same boy bugler who'd been leading Wellington in the streets of Washington two years earlier. Fought had, through his own wrangling, gotten himself attached to Custer as an orderly and the two were like brothers hardly inseparable. So it came as no surprise when Fought received a note summoning him to Headquarters. *"Someone said I was wanted at Headquarters (Pleasonton's.) It was a great surprise to see him (Custer) there. He said 'I am going to be right here, and I want you with me.'"*[33]

The New Commander of the Army of the Potomac
General George Gordon Meade

At about 3 PM on June 28th, Custer was called to the *"room"* of Major General Alfred Pleasonton inside the City Hotel in downtown Frederick, Maryland. It was here he received his promotion to the rank of Brigadier General and was given command of the Michigan Cavalry Brigade. *"I was never more surprised than when I was informed of my appointment as Brigadier General,"* wrote Armstrong, *"It was a position I had never in the faintest measure asked for. I felt highly complimented but had not the most remote idea that the President would appoint me, because I considered my youth, my low rank and what is of great importance at times I recollected that I had not a single friend at court."*[111]

35

*Later, his appointment or commission came
in the War Department envelope[94]
Captain Custer and his dog Rose*

Custer had been given command of the Michigan Cavalry Brigade, the unit was made up exclusively of men all from the same state. These volunteers under the guide of Custer would soon become the élan of the Union Army and a threat to the Confederate Cavalry under their best horseman, J.E.B. Stuart. They had been on the road since Thursday, the 25th of June, when they crossed the Potomac at Edwards Ford. On Friday 26th they reached Frederick, Maryland and went into camp remaining through Sunday June 28. Posted on the outskirts of town on York Pike Rd, they got word of the new commander of the army.

Born in Cadiz, Spain, General George Gordon Meade, a West Pointer graduating 19th in the class of 1831, was now assigned to the Command of the Army of the Potomac. Reluctantly accepting the position he now meticulously prepared to strike the Rebel line of advance in South East Pennsylvania and Lee accepted the challenge and gauge of battle.[83]

Into Pennsylvania, Lee had marched west from Fredericksburg through the gaps of the Blue Ridge Mountains into Maryland. He had intended to attack and capture Harrisburg thus cutting the Union in half.[82]

On the evening of June 28th Lee retired early and around 10:00 PM he was awakened by word that a civilian scout in Longstreet's employ named Harrison had reported that the Union Army had crossed the Potomac and was headed in their general direction. A collision would probably occur near a town called Gettysburg. Lee felt that it would be the place for a general engagement, Longstreet disagreed. *"If the enemy is there, we must attack him."*

"if he is there," retorted Longstreet, *"it will be because he is anxious that we should attack him-a good reason, in my judgment, for not doing so."*

That same day Stuart, who'd lost his bearings, had crossed the Potomac and arrived on the outskirts of Rockville, Maryland. Unaware of Stuart's presence, an enormous Federal supply train was simultaneously passing through the area. Insuffienctly protected, it was ripe for the picking. Within a short time 400 Union soldiers found themselves prisoners, and Stuart's cavalry was now in the moving business. Encumbered by the 125 captured wagons, supplies of sugar, hams and whiskey, JEB continued moving in the direction of Frederick, in hopes of linking up with Lee. A worried Lee, hoping to form a plan, was becoming distraught at not having heard from the *"eyes and ears"* of the Confederate Army.[95]

Errol Flynn as G.A. Custer in "They Died With Their Boots On"
Courtesy of john Langellier

Stuart's Adjutant, Henry McClellan frustrated by delays and cantankerous mules, realized the wagon train had become a burden, taking up miles of road and slowing the column considerably, suggested they burn 'em. Stuart rejected the idea, maintaining the importance of these very special supplies and he continued to push onward demanding the wagon train remain intact.[106]

The next thing we're told comes straight out of Hollywood via the film *"They Died With Their Boots On."* Stuart is at Hanover and Heaven help us, all that stands between him and Washington is *"The most irresponsible, incompetent, rattle brain 2nd Lieutenant in the Union Army"* who has been erroneously promoted to Brigadier General and put in command of the Michigan Brigade.

He arrives on the scene in an outlandish get up that can only be described as having *"more gold braid on him than a French Admiral!"* The only truth, is Hollywood's version of the uniform, although not quite right portrays the astonishment of such a uniform at first sight.

How was it that Captain George Armstrong Custer receives a summons from General Pleasonton on June 28th and by the 29th he is reviewing his troops at Richfield wearing what is undoubtedly the most elaborate and most detailed uniform in the whole Union Army?

A couple of weeks earlier he had written his Sister Ann, *"...In Case anything happens to me, my trunk is to go to you."*

What was in the trunk that he felt a need that it should go directly to his half-sister?

Granted there were letters he felt were sacred, but could there have been a uniform? A very special uniform she'd made for him? Similar to the one she'd made for him long ago when he was a small child in New Rumley, Ohio?

Custer's portrait, courtesy of Custer Battlefield Museum

Family tradition holds that Autie used to drill with the New Rumley Invincibles, the local militia commanded by his father. A small wooden rifle or wooden sword were part of his accoutrements as well as a smart uniform sewn by both his mother and half sister Lydia Ann.

Was the Custer humor still intact when he went canvassing the Michigan Regiments several weeks prior to his promotion hoping they would sign a petition to promote him to the rank of Colonel and possibly allow him to command one of the newly formed volunteer cavalry regiments of the Michigan Brigade? By chance might he have had a special uniform stored in his trunk recently sent to him via his sister Ann?

The galloons fastened to the sleeves were indicative to the rank of a Colonel in the Union Army although patterned closer to the design of Confederate Officers. The buttons were spaced for a Brigadier General, but until Joseph Fought , "...*found an old Jew and in his place he had a box of things belonging to a uniform and some stars. I bought two, then went back and found the Captain in his room at headquarters. I sewed them on, one on each corner of his collar. The next morning he was a full-fledged Brigadier General*"[94] Later two gold stars were sewn to the shoulders of the velveteen jacket.

Fought described the outfit as such: "*He wore a velveteen jacket with five gold loops on each sleeve, and a sailor shirt with a very large collar that he got from a gunboat on the James. The shirt was dark blue, and with it he wore a conspicuous red tie-top boots, a soft hat, Confederate, that he had picked up on the field, and his hair was long and in curls almost to his shoulders.*"[33]

Frederick Whittaker would write: "*...Custer managed to produce one of the most brilliant and showy dresses out of the hideous uniform, and to*

fashion it so that no one could mistake his rank. The regulation hat was a soft felt abomination, redolent of reminiscences of Praise-God Barebones and the Rump Parliament. The crown cut down, the brim widened, it became, on Custer's head, the veritable headgear of Prince Rupert, a regular cavalier hat, exactly suited to the long fair curls of the wearer. The custom of the service allowed a cavalry officer to wear a tight jacket instead of a coat. Custer wore a loose one. Velveteen was growing not uncommon for trousers, on account of its strength. Custer had both jacket and trousers made of it, to give richness of effect. Officers were permitted to wear on the sleeves of their overcoats, certain stripes of black braid to indicate their rank, when epaulettes and shoulder-straps were hidden. Custer put the braids in gold lace on his jacket sleeves, till they covered him nearly to the shoulder. A blue shirt with a broad falling collar, bore on its corner the silver star of a

The Uniform made famous by the Boy General photo courtesy of Dave Ingall

brigadier, and high boots, into which the loose trousers were thrust, completed the costume. He looked as if he had just stepped out of one of Vandyke's pictures, the image of the seventeenth century."[90]

Colonel Theodore Lyman of General Meade's staff exclaimed, "This officer is one of the funniest-looking beings you ever saw, and looks like a circus rider gone mad!...He wears a hussar jacket and tight trousers, of faded black velvet trimmed with tarnished gold lace. His head is decked with a little gray felt hat; high boots and gilt spurs complete the costume, which is enhanced by the General's coiffure, consisting in short, dry, flaxen ringlets!"[95]

"The first time I saw Custer was when we arrived at Hanover," remembered Captain Ballard. "When I first saw him he was about 6 foot 1 in height, smooth-faced, except for the long mustache, and with long golden hair, hanging on his shoulders for about a foot or 18 inches. When he was riding it was always flowing in the wind. He generally wore a black velvet jacket and tight black velvet breeches, top-boots, and long spurs, and he generally rode a horse that was fully the height of all men of his size. He wore the insignia of his rank on his sleeve, not on the shoulder. He also wore a white slouch hat and was a very striking-looking man. He was one of those men who, when you saw him pass at a gallop, you instinctively turned to look again."[62]

Amstrong with Alfred Pleasonton

Joseph Fought

After his meeting with General Pleasonton on June 28 at the City Hotel in Frederick, Maryland, Armstrong immediately took off with two buglers (Joseph Fought Co. D 5th U. S. Cavalry and Peter Boehn, Co. B 5th U. S. Cavalry)and a cadaverous waif named Johnnie Cisco, who'd attached himself to Armstrong, cared for his horses and dog Rose, and generally acted as his man servant.[33, 80] When then, would he have had time to put together his elaborate velveteen uniform?

Bob Servacek believes, and so do I, that Joseph Fought would have written about procuring the jacket and trousers. He'd gone into detail about sewing the stars to the corners of Custer's sailor shirt. So where had it come from? The uniform, simply, was already in his trunk when he arrived in Frederick, Maryland. The uniform and manner of his dress brought him attention. At first ridicule, but in time, the Brigade came to accept him and *Believe in the Bold*. The Red Tie, Autie's favorite color, became his trade mark. It also made an excellent target for a crack Confederate unit with explicit orders to take him out. If he'd not been an excellent horseman and constantly on the move, that unit would have drawn bead and certainly finished him off before the legend of the Boy General even began.

On Monday the 29th, a portion of The Michigan Brigade returned to Emmitsburg, Maryland en route they met up with General Custer. The 1st and 7th then went into camp at Richfield. Following a review, ever mindful of the horses' comfort, Armstrong , who to some seemed aloof and cold, inspected each company's mounts. He made certain there were no saddle sores, boils or sore feet. He inspected the [59] saddle bags to make certain each carried the extra horse shoes that were required and sporadically checked the horses teeth instructing the company farriers to float those that needed tending at the earliest possible opportunity. There had been an outbreak of Epizootic Catarrh, and he wanted to cull and quarantine any animals that might spread the infection. He asked for and was specific about weekly reports that he would require at headquarters describing the horses and condition of the men.

He had replaced Brigadier General Joseph T. Copeland, and this Brigade, from the start, was going to be run differently and by a man who knew and cared about horses. The confidence and trust bestowed upon him made Armstrong determined that the Michigan Cavalry Brigade was going to be the best in the service.

And, indeed, they would. He was now the youngest General in the Union Army. A General at age 23, Custer took command of the 1st, 5th, 6th and 7th Michigan, the 2nd Brigade of the 3rd Cavalry Division: the greatest light cavalry unit of its day.

The 5th and 6th would soon meet up with him at Hanover on the battlefield. By now the complexion of the Brigade was as follows:

Col. Charles H. Town commanded the veteran unit of the 1st Regiment consisting of 11 Companies; Col. Russell A. Alger's 5th Regiment was composed of 10 Troops; Col. George Gray headed up 10 Troops of the 6th Michigan and Col. William D. Mann's 7th Regiment also consisted of 10 Companies. Lt. Alexander C. M. Pennington Light Battery "M" 2nd U. S. Artillery commanded about 120 men who manned the six three-inch rifled ordnance guns that had seen service from Bull Run to Brandy Station. They added the punch to the Brigade.[69] But it was the Spencer Repeating Rifles that would prove the equalizers.

IV

"Hanover and Black Horse Cavalry"

Custer portrait courtesy of Custer Battlefield Museum

"If you want to catch the devil-
If you want to have fun-
If you want to smell hell-
Jine the Cavalry!"[118]

And *"jine he did,"* when seventeen year old Herbert Shriver, son of a Southern sympathizer, volunteered to escort Stuart and his enormous supply train captured at Rockville around Littlestown where federal troops were known to be riding, he was promised by Stuart an admission into Virginia Military Institute. Shriver's task, although tenuous, was greatly influenced by the terrain which impacted the movement of the supply train. Gaps between the front and rear units still caused anxiety, but Captain

William W. Blackford remarked on the benefit to the horses the captured supply wagons had with the additional oats. *"After giving my horses all they could eat I slung half a bag, saddle-bag fashion, across my saddle for future use, and my horse seemed to know what this additional load was, for he occasionally turned an affectionate glance towards it."*[108]

Previous to *"June 29th. We marched back from Emmettsburg."* wrote Colonel Russell Alger, Regimental Commander of the 5th Michigan, one of the very units Stuart was trying to elude. *" During the day General Copeland was relieved of his command, which was turned over to me temporarily. June 30th. We marched to Littletown, Pa, where the Michigan Cavalry Brigade, being 2d brigade, 3rd cavalry division, Army of the Potomac, consisting of the 1st, 5th, 6th, and 7th Michigan Cavalry, and Captain Pennington's battery of the U. S. Regular Artillery, was formed and placed under the command of Brigadier General G. A. Custer.*

From Littletown we marched to Honover Pa, where my regiment had its first serious encounter with the enemy..."[60] On Tuesday afternoon of June 30, 1863 the Michigan Cavalry Brigade pitched into Rebel forces under Major General JEB Stuart near Hanover, Pennsylvania. It had certainly not been Stuart's objective to engage anyone. He was on his 6th day of what he thought might be a ten-day ride. He wanted to pass through Hanover and go north through the Pigeon Hills in order to link up with the Confederate Corps of Richard Ewell. Most of the town's 1,700 residents: carriage makers, tobacco processors, smiths, clockmakers, weavers and iron molders, had already vacated for the second time in a few days when word came that *"The Rebels were coming, AGAIN!"* Three days earlier Confederates had come through burning bridges and cutting telegraph wires.[61]

J.E.B. Stuart. Artist F. Andrea

Around 8:00 AM on the 30th, General Kilpatrick's Union Division came thundering into town. He and the newly appointed Brigadier, George Custer, rode up Frederick Street at the head of the 1st and 7th Michigan Volunteer Regiments. When they reached the town square, they were enthusiastically greeted by some of the remaining townsfolk who passed coffee, fresh meat and pies amongst the troops who remained mounted.[161] After a short rest Kilpatrick sent Custer toward Abbottstown. For the moment, Kilpatrick intended to wait for Farnsworth's arrival and hoped to plug the route north through the Pigeon Hills with elements of the Third Cavalry Division. Almost an hour had passed since the Michigan Brigade had departed when Farnsworth and staff came cantering into Hanover. They were in kind treated as the men before them and much needed supplies and foodstuff passed to his troops. As the provisions were being distributed word arrived that the rear guard, about 40 men under Lieutenant Henry Potter of the 18th Pennsylvania, were under attack just west of town where the Confederates had set up two cannons and owing to the sudden attack, the Tar Heels were able to drive the 18th back into the town proper.[105]

43

By now, Stuart, who had no intention of getting into a battle in Hanover, came to the realization he needed to engage the Union forces with his three brigades of cavalry, while he quickly determined an alternate route to the north. At present, General Wade Hampton rode in the rear protecting the captured supply train. The 13th Virginia directed by Colonel John Chambliss, immediately drew sabres and charged the tail of the Yankee column successfully severing it in two and scattering the Union Cavalry in disarray about the center of town.[106] Hand to hand combat ensued through the streets resulting in over 300 casualties. The 2nd North Carolina, also of Chambliss' command losing nearly half of their effectives. During the melee local citizens began firing muskets and shotguns from the windows of their homes. For Lieutenant Potter, the cutting and slashing with sabres quickly changed, *"with those of us who were in the front it was a fist fight."*[108] Shortly, the 5th New York of Farnsworth's Brigade was able to rally and push the Confederates of John Chambliss out of town and onto the Rice and Keller Hills to the south.

At the initial contact, Kilpatrick sent word north to Custer who was within sight of Abbottstown when the fighting broke out.   When Custer received word from Kilpatrick, he immediately, *"Rode to the Sound of the Guns."* Coming on with all possible haste, spurring south and burning horse flesh to get there! Word was also sent east to the 5th and 6th Michigan Cavalry Regiments. These two regiments, part of Custer's brigade, had not linked up with the Boy General nor had they ever laid eyes on him. Both had held their own in a recent skirmish with Armstrong's old cavalry instructor from the Point, Fitzhugh Lee. The nephew of Robert E. Lee, Fitz had encountered the two Yankee regiments in his first fight since crossing into Pennsylvania.[115] Back at Hanover, Farnsworth's Brigade made up of the 18th Pennsylvania, 5th New York, 1st Vermont and the 1st West Virginia still engaged was forced to carry the fight for the better half of the conflict.

It had been *"Black Horse Cavalry"* that was so decisive in the Confederate victory two years before at Bull Run. Stories had been perpetuated about, *"the prowess of the Rebels. The Black Horse Cavalry* *were like demons mounted upon fiery dragons, and their swords fearful to think of."* [28] Now under the command of Colonel W. H. Payne, they struck the rear and flank of the Federals riding up Frederick Street. The 18th Pennsylvania Cavalry, in the confusion, made a disorderly retreat and scattered, while Stuart found himself all alone and directly in front of the charging Union Cavalry on the south end of town. With Farnsworth's cavalry in hot pursuit, he pulled up, drew his sabre and with a merry laugh spurred his favorite mare *"Virginia"* into an all out canter to get away. Clearing a hedge he made for a huge fifteen foot gully, *"I turned my head"* wrote Captain William Blackford, *" to see how Virginia had done it, and I shall never forget the glimpse I then saw of this beautiful animal away up in mid-air over the chasm and Stuart's fine figure sitting erect and firm in the saddle."*[89]

Understanding the size and strength of a horse is a humbling experience. A good horseman is always humble. If you're not at first, a horse will make you humble. And usually very quickly.

Colonel Payne was not quite so fortunate; finding himself separated from his unit and escorting a Union prisoner to the rear, the dismounted cavalryman grabbed a discarded rifle making an attempt to escape and unceremoniously shot Payne's horse dumping the Confederate Colonel into a tannery vat. The Union Cavalryman, Abram Folger, now had the drop on Payne and the pleasure of relating the dilemma of his new prisoner in *"his gray uniform with its velvet facing and white gauntlet gloves, his face and hair had all been completely stained, so that he presented a most laughable sight."*[61, 110] With the capture of their commander, the 2nd North Carolina retired from the field. Leaving the captured wagon train 2 miles out of town Hampton rushed onto the scene. Captain James Breathed and Captain William McGregor's Batteries unlimbered their six guns and began a two hour bombardment of the Union positions, indiscriminately targeting the town.[108]

Now it only remained for Custer to become engaged. He arrived with the 1st and 7th Michigan and attacked the Tar Heels at Rice and Keller Hills south of town. He is steady and resolute. The

Seventh, "...having the advance of the brigade in its rapid return from Abbottstown, was thrown into position on the left of the turnpike, to the left and front of Battery 'M' 2d U. S. Artillery. Two squadrons were dismounted, and advanced as skirmishers under the command of Lieutenant-Colonel Litchfield. In the progress of the action, the regiment was moved to the right of the town as a support to Battery 'M.' The skirmishers, having advanced beyond the town and exhausted their ammunition, were withdrawn. About five o'clock in the afternoon Companies 'C,' 'H," and 'E,' under command of Major Newcombe, were sent to occupy the town, which they took possession of and held until night, when the enemy withdrew."[104] Dismounted troopers of the 5th and 6th Michigan having arrived from Littlestown, now combined with the rest of the Brigade and fought as skirmishers surging across a ripening wheat field on the Karle Forney Farm. Custer all the while remained mounted directing them forward from the rear. "... we received orders to dismount to fight action front. As this was our first order of the kind, and came so suddenly, we were somewhat flustered, officers and men, but we were quickly in line, leaving every fourth man to care for the horses. The line advanced in good style, met the rebs, and after a short time beat them back, when we mounted and followed on a charge through Hanover. This was our first skirmish, and without loss, except Captain Dutcher, wounded."[103]

"As the men of the Sixth, armed with Spencer rifles, were deploying forward across the railroad into a wheatfield beyond, I heard a voice new to me, directly in rear of the portion of the line where I was, giving directions for the movement, in clear, resonant tones, and in a calm, confident manner, at once resolute and reassuring. Looking back to see whence it came, my eyes were instantly riveted upon a figure only a few feet distant, whose appearance amazed if it did not for the moment amuse me. It was he who was giving the orders. At first, I thought he might be a staff officer, conveying the commands of his chief. But it was at once apparent that he was giving orders, not delivering them, and that he was in command of the line." Captain James H. Kidd of the Michigan Cavalry Brigade in "Personal Recollections of A Cavalryman" described such a hero: "The Michigan men, with the exception of the 1st Cavalry, never had been under fire. It was their first battle. Suddenly, there appeared upon the scene a picturesque figure whom none of them had ever seen...an officer superbly mounted who sat his charger as if 'to manor born.'

'Custer at Hanover' By Artist Dale Gallon. Image courtesy of Gallon Historical Art. www.gallon.com

Tall, lithe, active, muscular, straight as an Indian and as quick in his movement, he had the fair complexion of a schoolgirl. He was uniformed in a suit of black velvet, elaborately trimmed with gold lace, which ran down the outer seams of his trousers and almost covered the sleeves of his cavalry jacket. The wide collar of a blue navy shirt with embroidered stars at the points, was turned over the collar of his velvet jacket, and a necktie of bright crimson was tied in a graceful knot at the throat, the long ends falling carelessly in front...A soft black hat with a wide brim...turned down on one side, giving him a rakish air. His golden hair fell...to his shoulders and his upper lip was garnished with a blonde mustache. A sword and belt, gilt spurs and top boots completed his unique outfit."[5]

The "First Michigan of my command," Custer confidently directed," was ordered to support Battery M, Second U. S. Artillery," from a place called Bunker Hill "at the Hanover engagement. No loss was sustained, as this regiment was not actually engaged. Fifth Michigan was also in the fight but suffered no loss. Sixth Michigan Cavalry drove the enemy to their guns, which we found supported by a heavy force of cavalry. A sharp engagement followed, in which we were outnumbered by the enemy six to one. This regiment lost 15 captured. Battery M, Second U. S. Artillery, under my command, while between Hanover and Abbottstown, had a chest of one caisson explode, mortally wounding one man and killing 2 horses."[105] Left only to take the Confederate cannon situated on the Jacob Forney Farm, they put up a galling fire, armed with their Spencer repeating rifles, purchased by the State of Michigan's Governor Austin Blair. The new rifle considered the most advanced state of the art weapon available, was christened the "*Spencer Repeater*" appeared on the scene in the late Spring of '63 and proved to be the premier small arm of the war.

Invented on his own time while working for the Sharps Firearms Company, Christopher Miner Spencer, who was born in Connecticut, was 20 years old when he received a patent on March 6, 1860 for a new repeating rifle. Self contained this lever action rolling block weighed about 8 3/4 lbs and fired a seven shot .52 calibre round housed in a magazine tube that was placed in the butt of the rifle's wooden stock. A spring in the magazine tube forced the next round into the chamber when the lever action swung down from the trigger at the same time ejecting the spent cartridge from the breech. An experienced soldier could chamber and fire up to seven shots in about fifteen seconds.[107] The Northern Army quickly purchased 12,471 rifles that were made in an old defunct piano factory in Boston, Massachusetts.[55,56,57] The first delivery was

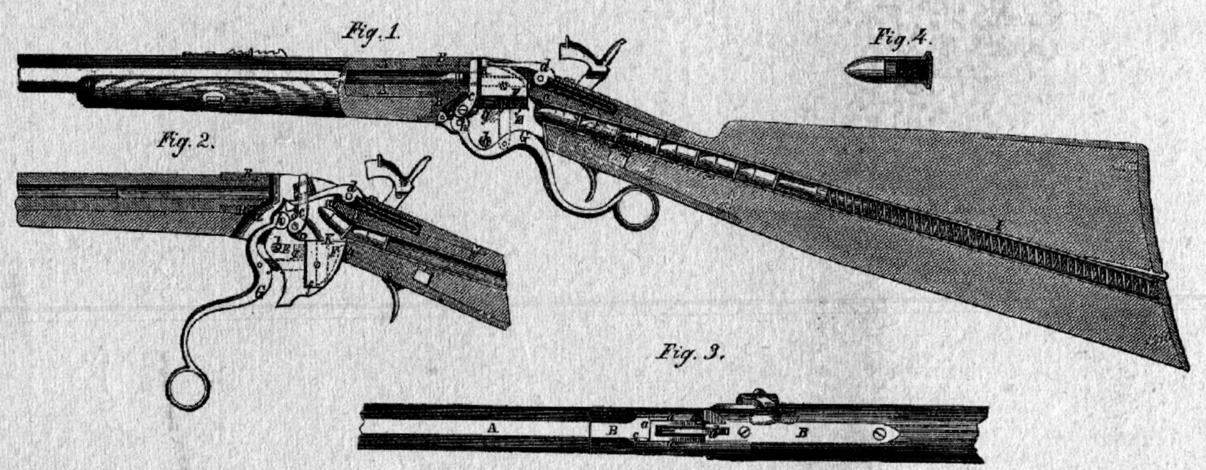

Mechanical workings of Spencer Repeater

made of 7,500 Spencer Rifles in December of '62. The Fifth Michigan received 500 outfitting all companies but K and E. By January an additional 300 arrived at "*Camp Copeland*" the Fifth given priority of the bulk of the rifles while a smattering of companies of the Sixth Michigan were armed with about 300 of the repeaters.[59,73]   Most of the Brigade was armed as follows:

The First Michigan Cavalry in late 1862 received .[52] caliber Sharps Breech-loading carbines, .[54] caliber Burnside Breech loading carbines and the .[44] Colt Army Model revolvers. They were called the Sabre Regiment as they were the veteran unit. The Fifth Michigan were armed with .[52] caliber Spencer repeating rifles and a brace of .[44] Colt pistols but no sabres. The Sixth Michigan came into service in October of 1862 being supplied with the .[44] Colt Army Revolver and Light Cavalry Sabre. And the Seventh Michigan had in their possession .[54] caliber Burnside Breech-loading carbines, .[44] caliber Colt Army revolvers and both light and regular sabres.[60]

It would be this devastating Spencer Rifle that turned the tide and forced the Confederate Artillery to abandon their pieces in Forney Field.[107] The battle continued to rage for 10 hours; Frederick Street being the main avenue of this urban battle with continuous shells dropping into homes and businesses in Hanover. Hours and hours of hand to hand fighting with sabres and revolvers leaving 27 dead horses laying all along Frederick Street. Stuart's troops over the course of the battle were able to capture over 400 horses to add to their remuda of over 1,000. These horses and the wagon train ultimately added to the burden of over 117 casualties lost in the engagement and proved to be little more than a nose tweaking but forced Stuart's Black Horse Cavalry further east delaying his arrival in Gettysburg until the evening of July 2.

A Couple of Michigan Cavalry Brigade Troopers with their Spencer Rifles

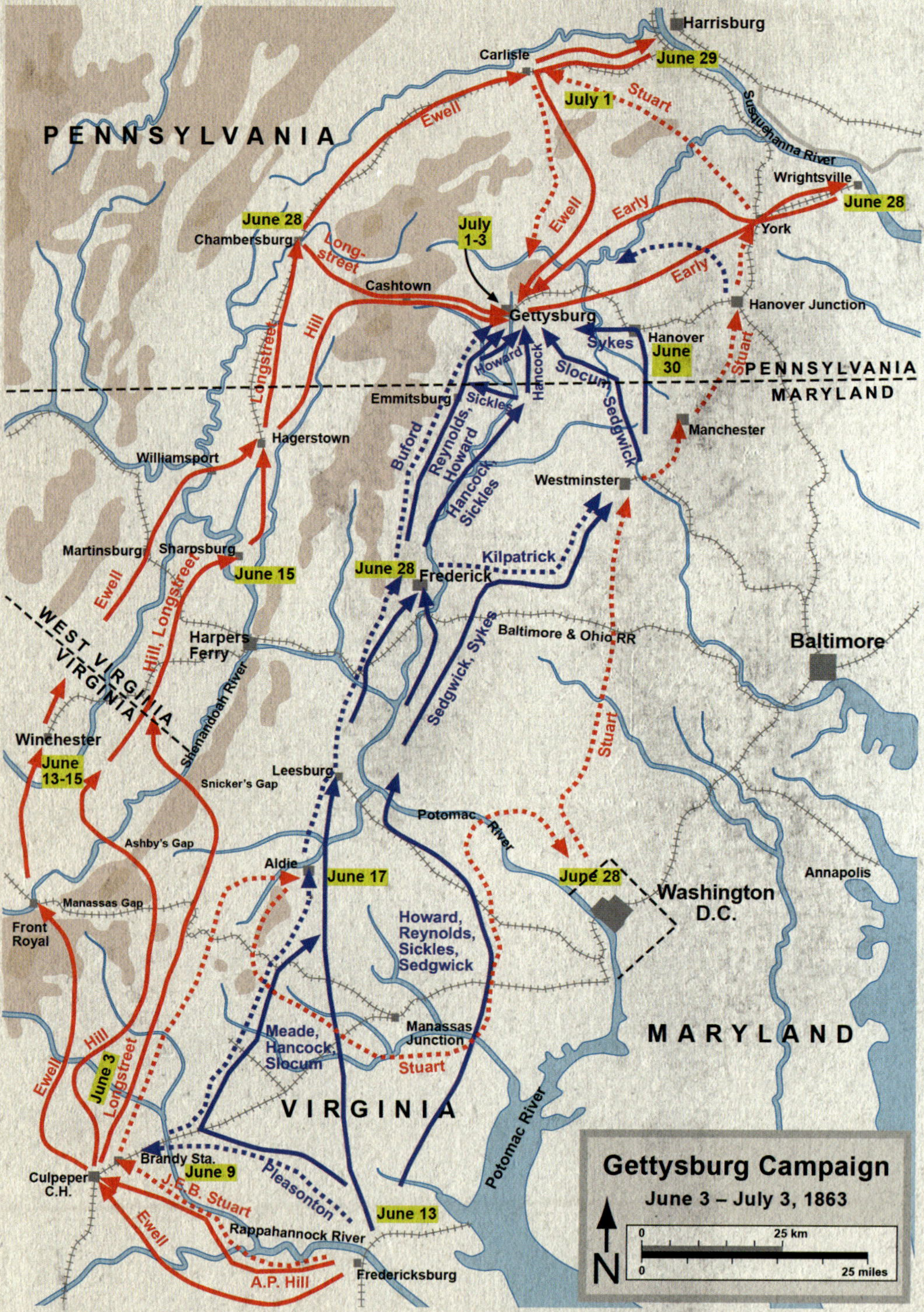

Map of the Battle of Gettysburg by Hal Jespersen

By now field intelligence was coming into Union High Command. General Pleasonton was pleased to hear of the Cavalry's success . Total Union casualties topped 200 but once again they had retained the field while the Confederates had made a quiet but organized withdrawal. Couriers from General Buford revealed disconcerting reports that the natural east-west route from Pittsburgh to Philadelphia running through the village of Hunterstown remained "*Infested*" with enemy pickets. Meade's overall concern was that the supply routes to the east might be compromised by this development. So when orders came from Division Commander, General Judson Kilpatrick, to continue covering the Union's right flank against Confederate attack, the Michigan Cavalry Brigade having experienced the "*Boy General's*" prowess under fire responded completely behind the general with the flowing locks.

Suspecting that there were the much needed supplies including a cache of badly needed shoes, Confederate General Henry Heth of A. P. Hill's Corps retorted, "*If there is no objection, General, I will take my division tomorrow and go to Gettysburg and get those shoes.*" [112] Given the go ahead he penetrated Gettysburg and was met by a Union Cavalry patrol approaching the town from the south on June 30th.[83] Lee's admonition to not engage until his army was concentrated on Cashtown Gap causing Hill to retire to the outskirts, determined to attack in force the following day. On July 1, the Confederates ran into stiff opposition when Buford's full Division arrived and deployed as dismounted skirmishers. General Buford was able to sustain and hold a position until Armstrong's old Commandant of Cadets, General John Reynolds who was rushing in with the 1st Corps of Infantry was shot and killed. Reynolds's presence inspired the troops, but his daring display in a forward position cost him his life when a Confederate sniper shot him out of the saddle.

Union General Howard's troops moved forward causing Heth's division to be momentarily forced back until Rebel General Robert Rode's division unexpectedly hit the right flank of the Federal Army on Oak and McPherson Ridge. With the arrival of Confederate General Jubal Early's division, mass panic enveloped the Union defense and a disorganized retreat through the streets of Gettysburg occurred eventually stabilizing on Cemetery Ridge. [82]

When Lee arrived he established strategic positions below the town on Seminary Ridge and in the hills and fields south and westerly, but instructed General Richard Ewell to capture Cemetery Hill "*if practicable.*" Second guessing his commander Ewell did not press the initiative. The first day ultimately belonged to the south, with demoralized and routed Federal troops fleeing through the streets of Gettysburg before rallying in the heights south of town and strengthening their position through the night.

Amazingly seventy-two year old John Burns a civilian in Gettysburg hearing the gun fire and confusion donned his best clothes and grabbed an old flintlock musket and walked out to join the Union troops fighting west of town.[83] He would fight the remainder of the battle emerging the "*Celebrated Civilian Hero of Gettysburg.*" On the first day of July, Custer was dispatched to assist Kilpatrick in repelling an assault of Wade Hampton's brigade of cavalry on East Cemetery and Culp's Hill.[53] Although they left Hanover during the early morning hours again marching north toward Abbottstown, rumors proved unfounded; they did not engage and eventually turned back from Berlin where they went into Abbottstown and bivouacked for the night.[99]

V

"Ambush at Hunterstown"

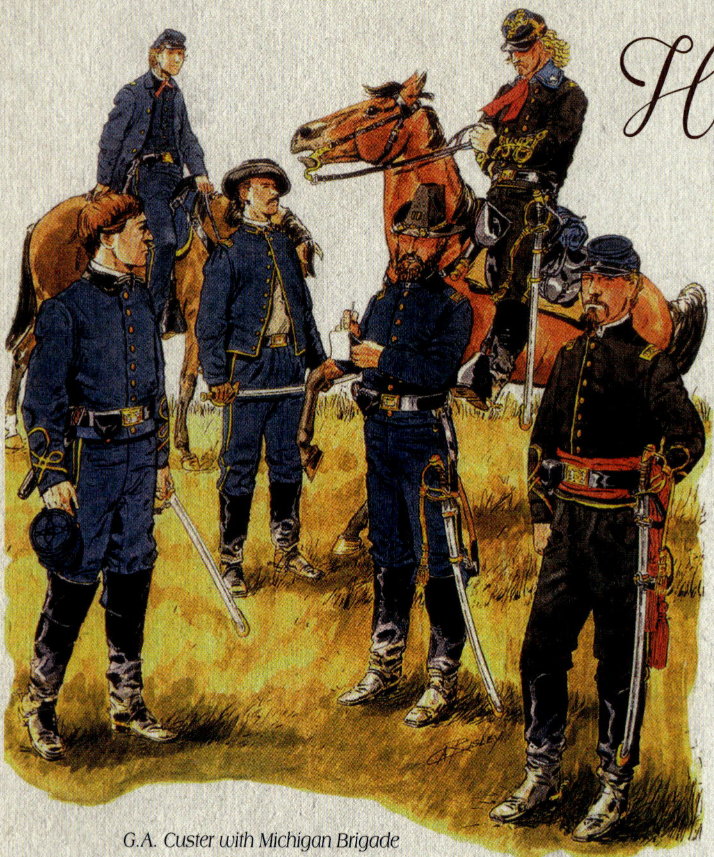

G.A. Custer with Michigan Brigade cavalry officers by A. Bisley.

"Cannon to right of them,
Cannon to left of them,
Cannon in front of them
Volley'd and thunder'd
Storm'd at with shot and shell,
Boldly they rode and well,
Into the jaws of Death,
Into the mouth of Hell...[63]

By July 2nd, things were escalating beyond anyone's imagination. Two Taverns and Hunterstown were receiving rapt attention from Pleasonton's staff. A detachment of Cobb's Legion had been in Hunterstown on June 28. Eighty-five men under Confederate Captain Crawford came to collect local horses for remounts and had informed the towns people that JEB Stuart was on his way. For the Confederate Cavalry, after more than two years of attrition, horse flesh was in short supply. Battle , disease and neglect had taken an uncalculable toll. Marches averaged about 12 miles a day and increased as the animals became toughened and more accustomed to campaigning. Daily rations for their horses should have been, and not always were, six pounds of grain per day. Marching orders were about four miles an hour and commenced at an easy walk for the first two miles, followed by a halt of about fifteen minutes to adjust saddles, packs and allow the horses to relieve themselves. A column on the move created an intoxicating sweet smell of manure and if the horses were healthy a halt of five minutes for each hour of march after that. After the first halt the speed of a column usually increased to about five miles an hour alternating between a walk and a trot given the terrain and obstacles permitting. On occasion especially when descending steep hills, dismounting and leading the horse was preferable relief both to the man and equine. Poor horsemanship as much as anything contributed to the damaging of the animals. At any given time there were about 60,000 horses servicing both armies. They required proper amount of grazing, water and care of their backs, feet and overall cleanliness. Horses needed a cooling off period preferably two miles before reaching camp. Since over heating became a factor, lines of march necessarily took into account water sources for both the men and the horses.[46] An officer of cavalry needed to be more a horse doctor than a soldier. On average a horse carried about 225 lbs. on his back. On active campaign he was saddled fifteen hours out of twenty four. The wear and tear to a horse's back sometimes caused his withers to swell three times the normal size with volcanic oozing sores. This and hoof problems could put a column out of commission and give an edge to the opposing forces. Procuring healthy relief mounts became a necessity more than a luxury and often times dictating the course of march in order to steal, beg or borrow from the citizenry.[108]

Besides being on the natural line of march toward Philadelphia, Hunterstown was positioned in such a fashion to be on a natural watershed and road system. The reputation of horse farms and other livestock made it particularly attractive to the raiding army and influenced their decision to veer off on their way to link up with Lee's main army.

Only two Union cavalry units were protecting General Dan Sickles and the Union Third Corps near the Round Tops. Sickles whose flamboyant lifestyle would get him into more difficulties than the largest battle on America's soil, was best remembered for successfully pleading a defense of temporary insanity, but on July 2, would lose a leg in the wheat field and have to be stretchered off while smoking his cigar commenting, *"In a war like this one, a man's life is of small account."*[117] Later he would periodically visit his amputated leg at the Army Medical Museum in Washington D. C. Realizing the necessity of higher ground Union, General Gouverneur Warren pushed for and secured Little Round Top before Confederate troops who were eyeing that position climbed to its heights. The signal station on Little Round Top had earlier observed 10,000 Confederates marching toward the likewise vulnerable Union right flank and the inevitable assault on Culp's Hill could have severed Meade's lines of communication and supply. Gregg's Cavalry Division was placed on Hanover Road and Kilpatrick was given the instructions, *"Prevent our right flank from being turned."* He rushed to stay the balance of power on the Hunterstown Road to the north.

By mid-afternoon he was in Hunterstown and had established headquarters in the Grass Hotel. This large beautiful structure became a hospital and within hours eight union soldiers would expire and be carried dead from there. Some will end up in graves outside the Great Conewago Presbyterian Church on the north side of town. From this temporary HQ/Hospital Kilpatrick sent a message to Armstrong: *"4 P.M., July 2 Custer-Ewell is knocking hell out of Howard on Culp's Hill. If H.(oward) cannot hold ground, we are flanked. Cut E(well)'s communications; harass his rear; at all hazards, relieve pressure on H(oward).- Kilpatrick"*[113] If Culp's Hill fell to the south, virtually the entire Union battle line along Cemetery Ridge would be subject to indefensible rear gunfire from combined Confederate troops. [119]

"We struck Hunterstown within, I guess, 8 miles from Gettysburg," remembered Lt. Stephen Ballard, of the 1st Michigan. The Hunterstown Road from the constant pounding of wagon, cannon and horse had become a dry gray powdery dust. Almost the same consistency of talc powder. The puffs and clouds kicked up by the forward horses were irritating to the eyes and parching the throats of the enlisted as they made their way south to get into position. The Sixth was tasked to enter the town from the east and soon encountered Colonel Pierce Manning Butler Young's rebel vedettes, who fell back through the village joining the Confederate defense about a mile southwest of town.[122] Young who'd been a classmate of Autie's at the Academy had forewarned *"Custer, my boy, we're going to have war. It's no use talking; I see it coming. All the Crittenden compromises that can be patched up won't avert it. Now let me prophesy what will happen to you and me. You will go home, and your abolition Governor will probably make you a colonel of a cavalry regiment. I will go to Georgia, and ask Governor Brown to give me a cavalry regiment. And who knows but we may move against each other during the war. You will probably*

Preliminary study for
"I'll Lead You This Time"
by Jared Frederick
www.historymatters.biz
Courtesy of Roger and Laurie Harding

get the advantage of us in the first few engagements, as your side will be rich and powerful, while we will be poor and weak. Your regiment will be armed with the best weapons, the sharpest sabres; mine will have only shotguns and scythe blades; but for all that we'll get the best of the fight in the end, because we will fight for a principle, a cause, while you will fight only to perpetuate the abuse of power." [123]   On this day both would test their mettle in the war that pitted brother against brother and made foes of friends. In May of '63 Armstrong came into possession of a beautiful black gelding he called *"Harry"* named for his nephew back home in Monroe, Michigan. The steed had carried him through the ensuing months prior to his promotion to Brigadier General and it was this same gelding Autie wheeled and spurred south down Hunterstown Road. The rolling road cut through farmland flanking each side of a split rail fence. The winter wheat had bearded out and although much of the plant remained green it would only be a matter of a few weeks before the Pennsylvania farmers would harvest it. Pulling up Harry, Armstrong stood up in his stirrups and quickly assessed the situation before him. In a manner of seconds he eased back into his McClellan saddle. His mind made up he began giving instructions to his troop commanders in the disposition of the troops. So quickly had he made these troops' deployment that some might call him impetuous or impulsive to which he later addressed: *"I am not impetuous or impulsive. I resent that. Everything that I have ever done has been the result of the study that I have made of imaginary military situations that might arise. When I become engaged in a campaign or battle and a great emergency arises, everything that I have ever heard or studied focuses in my mind as if the situation were under a magnifying glass and my decision was the instantaneous result. My mind works instantaneously but always as the result of everything I have studied being brought to bear on the situation."* [124]

And so his plan set he turned to Colonel Town of the 1st Michigan, *"... one squadron, under command of Captain Duggan, was detailed to hold the road leading into the town from the right front of it. One platoon was deployed as skirmishers on the left of the road leading into town from the rear. This platoon was actively engaged and did good service."* [121]   The remainder of the Brigade's advance to the south soon discovered the combined Confederate force made up of the 1st North Carolina and 2nd South Carolina Cavalries; thrown in also for good measure was Phillip's and Cobb's Georgia Legions falling into position behind a rail fence near the Gilbert Farm. By 5 PM Alexander Pennington's Battery M, 2nd U. S. Artillery has been unlimbered and set in position; fourteen paces between each gun and cloaked by a large barn on the Felty Farm. Every door and window now occupied by Michigan troopers, their Spencer rifles at the ready. Backed by the 1st and 5th in reserve Custer directed three companies of the 6th Michigan to fall in on foot west of the road. The 7th on the opposite side of the Hunterstown road dismounted and deployed in the wheat field totally hidden from the Rebel forces. Ordering Captain Henry Thompson Company A Sixth Michigan forward Custer shouted, *"I'll lead you this time, boys. Come on follow me!"*

"Custer gave us orders to charge down a little lane with one of those post and rail fences on each side of the road," remembered Lieutenant Ballard, like the confines of a bowling alley. In an instant sixty men, four abreast, drew sabres and in a flash cantered down Hunterstown Road all the while enclosed by rail fencing on each side; funneling , flailing and fatally floundering horse flesh as they banged up against the split rail fence flanking the road. Like a minie ball discharging from a rifled musket the sixty in what seemed like suicide slammed into more than six hundred. All the while Custer knowing the mindset of his Confederate adversaries would not turn away from such a challenge. [125]

Young Norvell Churchill

A death-raking volley erupted like the tearing of bed sheets, from the Confederate's position hitting Custer's horse. The Black gelding started to go down and while instantly kicking out of his stirrups, Armstrong prepared for the impact. Harry was dead by the time he collapsed on the ground. Autie had allowed the full force to be absorbed by the horse, rolling free and was quickly on his feet. A Confederate Cavalryman discovering the prone *"Boy General"* and Harry dead beside him, rode up to deliver the coup de grace with a raised sword. Just as the Confederate officer lunged forward to thrust a sword through the Golden Cavalier, the quick thinking Norvell Churchill, in a moment of extreme exuberance broke from Company L 1st Michigan riding in, placing himself between the Rebel and his General. He deflected the Rebel's sabre blow with his own sword, and then shot the Confederate officer point blank with his revolver. Shoving out his hand to the general, Custer leaped onto the croup of Churchill's saddle and the two rode out of harm's way. The momentum of the Rebel juggernaut carried them beyond the skirmish north into the unsuspected Union vortex. What was left of the 60 men of Custer's 6th Michigan continued their retreat drawing the Confederates into a trap. Custer's improvised Genghis Khan method of decoying the Confederates to pursue him back up Hunterstown road for the ambush, worked like a charm. Pierce Young and about 40 men fell victim to the Brigade which opened a deadly cross fire with Spencer rifles and double shot 3 inch Ordnance Guns, decimating the confined and confused frontal assault of Cobb's Legion. *"Our command had a thrilling experience,"* remembered Confederate Private Wiley Howard, *"while charging a body of cavalry down a lane leading by a barn, ran into an ambuscade of men posted in the barn who dealt death and destruction upon us. Within five minutes some four or five officers were killed or wounded and about fifteen men were slain or wounded."*[125, 126]

Original sketch by John Heiser and given to the author in 2010

Custer became unhorsed and Norvell Churchill intervened and saved his life.

At the head of the charging Confederates Lt. Col. Wm. Delony's prancing bay "*Marion*" was shot from under him. The Lt. Colonel's right collar bone was broken by sabre blows from 3 Union soldiers slashing down at him while he held up his left arm to deflect their chops and protect his head. Bugler Henry Jackson rode up holding out his bugle to deflect their sabre slashes. "*Jackson's bugle, coat and shirt were cut through with saber blows...*" Yet he managed to save Delony's life, but only for a few more months; Delony would fall at Jack's Shop, Virginia in September. The battle action continued to swirl between the Gilbert and Felty Farms until Hampton reinforced Young's men moving two Confederate pieces forward. Hampton then began an artillery duel that would last well into the twilight hours. Eventually, ordered to withdraw, Hampton retired from the field boosting the confidence of the New Brigade under the General with the Golden Locks. Stephen Ballard concluded, "*Still we hit them severely, for twenty-two dead were picked up, every one sabered.*"[52, 110, 127] *This is the Boy General's First Charge with the Brigade and they immediately admired him, "The command perfectly idolized Custer. The old Michigan Brigade adored its Brigadier, and all felt as if he weighed about a ton.*"[62]

Twenty-three-year-old, Norvell Churchill had become the hero of the day. Such was the jubilation for a small town farm boy who grew up in rural Almont, Michigan. Raised around thoroughbred horses, it was only natural that when war erupted in 1861 he would gravitate toward the Cavalry and eventually care for the horses of one of history's greatest cavalrymen.

55

In August of 1861, Churchill enlisted in Company L, 1st Michigan Cavalry. This veteran unit saw action almost immediately and gained a reputation as a Sabre Regiment. Within two years the 1st Michigan was thrown together with the 5th, 6th and 7th Michigan Cavalry Regiments to form the Michigan Cavalry Brigade. Under the command of General Joseph T. Copeland, the Brigade saw action in small skirmishes, but was unable to show their mettle in battle because the Union high command did not know quite how to use cavalry as an effective force. After the Confederate shellacking at Brandy Station and promotion of the Boy Generals, the Union Cavalry became an effective arm of the Union Army. July 2nd at Hunterstown only furthered the Federal thought that way.

Of Churchill, Custer would commend and mention his name in his official reports, *"I desire to commend to favorable notice Norvell Churchill, Company L, 1st Michigan..."* Churchill's *"remarkable gallantry"* earned him the appointment as one of Custer's special orderlies. Future engagements did not diminish his bravery and he was numerous times recommended for battlefield promotions, that he turned down. His own horse shot from under him, the ultimate care of the Custer's mounts became Churchill's responsibility. Norvell's son Hugh, remembers his father saying *"Custer's horses had the reputation for being the best fed in the cavalry."*[129]

Norvell's friendship with General Custer did not end with the war. Years later, *"After the war,"* remembers Hugh Churchill, *"Custer came to visit my father at his Romeo, Michigan farm"* Unable to persuade Norvell to accompany him west, the General *"stayed for three days before going off to the Indian Campaigns."*[130]

While Hampton's guns echoed near Hunterstown, the Confederates began a heavy bombardment in their attempt to take Culp's Hill. The Union responded in kind. Lt. Col. James Arthur Fremantle of the British Coldstream Guards, a foreign observer attached to Longstreet's Headquarters remarked, *"...in a few moments the firing along the whole line was as heavy as it is possible to conceive. A dense smoke rose for six miles; there was little wind to drive it away, and the air seemed full of shells."*[64] The main theatre of the battle would take place south of town; over 172,000 men and 634 cannon would engage in an area encompassing 25 square miles.[67] The Cacophony of the guns echoed and reverberated off the South Mountain, people in the towns of Pittsburgh and Harrisburg were able to hear the rolling reports of the guns. Confederate Artillerist Edward Porter Alexander would remember, *"I don't think there was ever in our war a hotter, harder, sharper artillery afternoon than this."*[42]

During this engagement, head of the Class of June, 1861 Twenty-six-year-old Patrick Henry O'Rorke fell on the rocky slopes of Little Round Top. Ordered by his math instructor from West Point General Warren to lead the 140th New York into the Wheatfield, Colonel O'Rorke, in a counter-attack that turned back four Rebel regiments, died instantly a bullet to the neck. Warren would later write, *"I would have died to save him."*[76] He is yet another of Armstrong's classmates from the Academy, that will be affected by this country torn asunder.

Since heavy guns relied on horse teams for mobility, destroying the teams of horses resulted in disabling the guns. By July 2, over 1,500 Artillery horses littered the field of conflict. Early in the onset of the war there were more horse causalities than troops and life expectancy for a horse was no more than six months. Flying Artillery relied on foam flecked teams to pull up to 3,800 lbs. The six-horse team would draw the cannon, limber and caisson and a single Battery might be manned by over a 100 troopers. Besides the driver and gun crew, who were often mounted on seperate or remount stock, the lead horses in the team might be ridden to aid the wheel or pole horses that particularly bore the brunt. Lead horses, slightly larger than cavalry mounts, were pampered and given special attention and care. Teams were seldom frightened if their drivers stayed beside them and reassured them during the loud bombardments.

The ability to wheel into position, unlimber, load and sight the cannon was only exceeded by the ability to remove the gun from the field. Often times the enemy having reduced or fully destroyed the team; now put the gun in jeopardy of capture, so the artillery crew would resort to the prolonged method, which utilized a long rope attached to the gun hitch that was either pulled manually or by one horse to draw it back from harm's way. Once the gun was discharged the slack in the rope was taken up, gun reloaded and the process continued until the gun was pulled to the protection of the rear.[92, 128]

"The night of July 2nd was spent devoted in great part to repairing damages, replenishing ammunition chests, and reducing and reorganizing such batteries as had lost so many men, equipment and horses..."[128]

Painting by W. H. Shelton

The author kneels at the Norvell Churchill's grave and holds the sabre of the man who saved Custer's Life.

Photographs courtesy of Daniel D. Dunn

Alexander marks Gettysburg anniversary

7-5-08

BY RONDA STIFFLER

In July, 1863, George A. Custer led his first charge as brigadier general at Hunterstown in Gettysburg. Monroe's "Sighting the Enemy" statue commemorates Custer's role in this battle.

The Hunterstown Historical Society is dedicating a monument honoring Pvt. Norvell Churchill, who saved Custer's life during the battle when the brigadier general's horse was shot and he was pinned beneath the animal's body.

"Pvt. Churchill rode in between a Confederate officer, who was wielding a blade, and Custer, pulling him to safety," said Mr. Alexander.

Norvell Churchill was born in Berlin Township. He joined Company L of the 1st Michigan Cavalry in 1861 and became an orderly to Custer shortly before the Battle at Gettysburg.

Mr. Alexander authored the text of the 5 foot by 4 foot memorial marker, the first historical marker of its kind to be placed at Hunterstown. The project was funded with money raised by the 3rd Michigan Infantry out of Grand

BACKGROUND

Local Gen. George A. Custer historian Steve Alexander recently completed his re-creation of the Army's 7th Cavalry's last ride but continues portraying Gen. Custer this week in Gettysburg for the 145th anniversary of the Civil War battle there.

Mr. Alexander is detailing his trip to Monroe writer Ronda Stiffler.

Rapids and the Hunterstown Historical Society under the leadership of Roger and Laurie Harding.

As the event's official Gen. Custer, Mr. Alexander also is appearing in re-enactments of the battles of Hunterstown, Hanover and Rimmel Farm while in Gettysburg.

Locally, he will portray Custer during the 2008 Custer Celebration in October. This year's theme centers on the general's family and friends and includes visits from Buffalo Bill Cody and Grand Duke Alexei Alexandrovitch Romanov re-enactors.

– Evening News file photo

George Custer leads the Michigan Cavalry Brigade in a diorama of third day of the Battle of Gettysburg.

DID YOU KNOW?

Three days before the Battle of Gettsburg, George Custer was promoted from captain to brigadier general and, at 23 years old, he became one of the youngest generals in the Union army.

During the battle, Custer led a mounted charge of the 1st Michigan Cavalry with his often repeated battle cry, "Come on, you Wolverines!"

Custer also played a significant role in the Battle of Hanover. Union troops were able to hold off the Confederate regiment, which delayed its attempt to rejoin Robert E. Lee's army.

Annual Hunterstown Festival held at the Tate Farm currently owned by Roger and Laurie Harding

Photo courtesy of Daniel D. Dunn

Live by the sword ... saved by the sword

— Photo courtesy of Darryl Wheeler/Gettysburg Times

The first monument to be erected honoring a little-known battle between two well-known protagonists of the American Civil War was dedicated last week in Hunterstown, Pa. The event marked the Battle of Hunterstown, between forces led by Union Brig. Gen. George Armstrong Custer and Confederate Gen. J.E.B. Stuart, just south of the village. Gathered around the monument are (from left) Hugh Churchill II, great-great-grandson of Pvt. Norvell Francis Churchill, the man credited with pulling Custer from the deadly advance of Confederate cavalry in the July 2, 1863, battle just south of the Village of Hunterstown; Hugh's father, Hugh Churchill; Monroe's Steve Alexander, portraying Gen. Custer, and Mike Wassuta of Tenafly, N.J., portraying Pvt. Churchill. Leaning against the stone marker is the sword Pvt. Churchill carried during the battle.

7-9-2008

MONUMENT WORDING

The monument says the following: "Three-fourths of a mile south of this site on the Hunterstown Road, newly appointed Brigadier General George Armstrong Custer led the Michigan Cavalry Brigade (1st, 5th, 6th and 7th Regiments) in his first charge against superior forces of Confederate cavalry under General Wade Hampton and Cobb's Legion on July 2, 1863. During the attack, Custer's horse was shot from under him. Without a horse but uninjured, he found himself prone to the mercy of Confederate blades that bore down on him. This decisive first encounter nearly proved fatal if not for the bravery and quick thinking of Norvell Francis Churchill, Company "L" 1st Michigan Cavalry, who deflected a saber blow and pulled the "boy general" to the back of his steed, extracting him from harm's way."

Monroe Evening News Wednesday July 9, 2008

VI

"Long Day at Rummel's Farm"

"Virginian blood runs in their veins,
And each his ardor scarce restrains;
Proud of the part they're chosen for:
The mighty cyclone of the war,"[65]

Sighting the Enemy
Sculptor, Edward Potter
Monroe, Michigan

Stuart's attempt to once again ride around the Union Army had caused delay in providing vital military information to General Lee. Anxiety compelled Marse Robert to reprimand him upon his arrival by mid-afternoon of July 2nd, *"Well General Stuart, you are here at last."* The next day *"Ole Jeb"* was destined to meet his opposite number. If not equaling him in cavalry tactics, most certainly in flamboyance would be George Armstrong Custer.

On July 2nd, Lee's plan to attack a simultaneous movement against both flanks was wrought with failure. On the night of the 2nd with additional Federal troops arriving the Union anchored the high water mark and transformed their defenses into the configuration of a giant *"fishhook."*[82]

After two days of previously probing the Union left flank then the right, Lee decided the weak link must be the center. His strategy was to throw his whole weight at the center, believing that the Union defenses had thinned out as they tapered toward each heavily fortified flank. An attack at that prone center would force Meade to draw troop strength from the flanks to reinforce the under siege center. Then, if a controversial distracting movement or an attack on each flank could be orchestrated, Meade would be forced to pull those reserves from the middle causing the center to be once again vulnerable. Custer, ever eager for a fight, later believed Stuart was to be the diversion on the flank while Lee attacked Cemetery Ridge.[120, 141] If this was the plan, it had every reason to succeed. Yet, Longstreet had objected to a plan like this and pushed that Lee needed to move around Meade's left flank, cut off all communications and force the Union to attack. Lee's probe around the left flank would put him on a course toward Washington, and Meade *"The Old Snapping Turtle,"*[83] would be hard pressed to intervene and stay the Confederates movement. Lee felt this would appear he was breaking off the engagement and withdrawing

James Ewell Brown Stuart

from the fight. He reasoned, that the fight must be won here on Northern soil and such a success at Gettysburg could mean foreign recognition of a legitimate Confederacy.[42]

Dawn broke July 3rd, with General Lee's decision to attack the Union defenses on Cemetery Ridge. Nine infantry brigades, close to 12,500 brave hearted Confederate troops under Major Generals George Pickett, Johnson Pettigrew and Isaac Trimble began a movement that would cross three-quarters of a mile long open rolling fields and orchards in one of history's most disastrous charges. Possibly coordinating with the assault, Stuart would surreptitiously attack the Union right flank.[141] Hopes were that the demoralized Federals would flee and their defenses buckle. Two days of fighting in the Wheatfield, Peach Orchard and Devil's Den had not fully determined the weakness in the Union line. Lee sought a major strategy and made plans to attack the Union center atop Cemetery ridge rightly thinking, *"If the troops I commanded could not take that position, all Hell couldn't take it."*

The day started with the fighting commencing first on Culp's Hill. After three days of the battle, the only civilian casualty occurred the morning of July 3rd, when a stray bullet entered the home of Georgia Wade McClellan on Baltimore Street, killing her sister, twenty-two year old Jennie Wade who was preparing biscuits for the troops in the kitchen.[83]

While Infantry on both sides slugged it out at Culp's Hill, Union high command did not miss recognizing the importance of the Hanover and Low Dutch Roads. Gregg decided to strongly picket it, deploying McIntosh and Col. J. Irwin Gregg's men to connect in a line with Infantry already in place at Wolf's Hill. Early in the morning of the third, Division Commander Judson Kilpatrick received orders to move his division to the Army's left flank and he ordered Custer and the Michigan Brigade to move at once and follow the 1st Brigade under Farnsworth towards Gettysburg. Custer's Wolverines had already been ordered northward to place the 2nd Brigade 3rd Cav. Div. in position on the pike leading from Hanover to Gettysburg. This position was on the extreme right of the Union forces. It would now be up to McIntosh to fill the gap left by the Michigan men. When Federal scouts on Cemetery Ridge observed Stuart moving on the York Pike with plans of turning the Union Right flank near Cress Ridge, General Gregg sent a courier to Custer asking him to return, adding his brigade to Gen. David McMurtie Gregg's 2nd Division composed of 2 brigades under Colonels John B. McIntosh and Irwin Gregg along with Captain Alanson Randol's single artillery Battery.[74, 75, 135] Dismounted scouts had just returned to report that they would be up against 4 Brigades and 3 Batteries under Stuart, Hampton and Fitzhugh Lee marshalling three miles east of the town of Gettysburg on Cress Ridge. Two brigades of cavalry; Black Horse Troop of Fauquier County, Virginia and Hampton's Legions, were part of Stuarts Invincibles all supported by artillery

were already moving through the trees to gain the higher ground. At noon The Michigan Brigade received the second order delivered by Pleasonton's aide-de-camp George Yates, to move out. Gregg immediately counter manned the order.

General Gregg recalled, "*At 12 m. I received a dispatch from the commander of the Eleventh Army Corps to the Major General commanding the Army of The Potomac, that large columns of the enemy's cavalry were moving to the right of our line...the enemy's cavalry gained our right and were about to attack, with the view of gaining the rear of our line of battle. The importance of successfully resisting an attack at this point, which, succeeded in by the enemy, would have been productive of the most serious consequences, determined me to retain the brigade of Kilpatrick's Division until the enemy were driven back. General Custer, commanding the brigade, fully satisfied of the intended attack, was well pleased to remain with his brigade...The very superior force of dismounted skirmishers of the enemy advanced on our left and front required the line to be reinforced by one of General Custer's regiments.*"[66]

"*About 1 o'clock there was such a crash of artillery as was never heard before on the Continent,*" Major Trowbridge of the 5th Michigan remembered.[116] In order to soften the Union center Lee began a bombardment with over 140 cannon.   "*The earth quaked,*" recalled Captain James Kidd. "*The tremendous volume of sound volleyed and rolled across the intervening hill like reverberating thunder in a storm.*"[157] One hundred Federal artillery pieces responded in kind beginning an hour and a half cannon duel. It ended only when Union General Henry Hunts' concern to conserve ammunition prevailed. While the guns cooled, Confederate Artillery Colonel E. P. Alexander mistakenly thought the Union guns had been silenced, taken out of commission and/or were out of shells.

Generals Pleasonton and Custer.   George Yates stands behind Alfred Pleasonton seated on the left.

After the war Yates would serve under Custer in the 7th U. S. Cavalry.

On Cress Ridge the Confederates opened the ball with four quick consecutive rounds from their Parrott rifles fired in the cardinal directions. This was a signal to Lee that Stuart was in position to attack in conjunction to the main assault on Cemetery Ridge. The courageous but futile attack known as *"Pickett's Charge"* could now commence.[114] At the Confederate cannon's belch, the younger horses in the Michigan Brigade spooked and almost dropped their riders. The 1st Sergeant calmly spoke up, *"Hold yer horses boys. They'll be plenty of Johnnies to Do-si-doe with."*

Roanoke the Iron Gray stallion who'd Custer captured on a raid in the Tide Water region of Virginia was his charger for the day. Roanoke at the first shell burst flared his nostrils and blew air, flinching only slightly sideways, before Armstrong was able to recover him slapping his gauntleted hand against the side of his neck. *"Easy boy."* He removed his glove and began pinching and rubbing Roanoke's neck in a circular motion as in the manner his mother had done nuzzling him when he was a colt. The stallion had a very impressive look to him; he was iron gray and although many cavalrymen shied away from that color claiming, *"They were too conspicuous…a gray horse that lies in muddy places is very apt to get dirty. If you were coming in from a night of picket duty, would you rather take a rest, or spend your time getting your horse ready for inspection?"* Though a dark coated horse might not show the mud so much, both Armstrong and Pleasonton were impressed with grays and Gray Eagle became Pleasonton's signature mount. Roanoke had a smooth and easy gait like a Tennessee Walker. He had a hard mouth and threw his head like an Arabian. Armstrong used a martingale and a firm hand. But the horse was steady under fire and would always perform given

his head. Roanoke twisted his neck to the left and looked for a moment into Custer's eye as if to say, *"You won't be getting us into a fix?"* Armstrong patted him reassuringly again and Roanoke swished his tail already resigned and comfortable with whatever his master chose for the moment.

The other horses on line stepped sideways and forward anxious for the occasion. Some pawing at the earth, others rubbing their faces on the troopers' legs beside them. Armstrong had reluctantly mounted Roanoke that morning due to the loss of Harry the day before.

Pennington then, advanced his caissons and unlimbered his guns; wheeling all six guns into position. In an all absorbing moment the Confederates drew sabres. There was the all too familiar *"Shiinng!"* as 4,000 blades cleared their metal scabbards. The midday sun cast a blinding reflection off their unsheathed blades. In the sea of bearded faces, weather worn hats and faded butternut and gray uniforms Armstrong's eye was drawn to a single individual. *"Sighting the Enemy"* he couldn't make out the facial features but he recognized his seat. The way he sat a horse. Armstrong had seen it a thousand times at the Academy. *"Fitz Lee,"* in the next breath an expletive escaped his lips. Colonel John McIntosh rode up to Armstrong saluting smartly and inquiring as to the enemy's status? Custer replied, *"I think you'll find the woods out there full of them."*[132]

Hardly had the words escaped his mouth when the enemy opened up with their battery of six guns. Their 10-pound Parrott Rifles, named after West Point graduate Robert Parker Parrott who invented the gun, could fire three 10 lbs. shells per minute. If they were able to see a target they could

Former Cavalry Instructor and Confederate General Fitzhugh Lee

battery weapon was as devastating as a 12-pound Napoleon and could send a projectile 1,850 yards, but preferred Schenkl shells known as shrapnel for maximum killing effect.[128] *"Well done,"* Pennington complimented his crew, *"Now try the left gun."* The next shot nearly three-fourths of a mile distance found its mark knocking the Confederate Parrott from its carriage. It had *"...struck the hub of the left wheel and exploded,"* Samuel Harris of the 5th Michigan would later write, *"disabling the gun and, as Pennington expressed it, sent six of the Rebel gunners to the happy hunting grounds."*[157] The second lucky shot had in fact, now caused the Rebels to withdraw their artillery pieces from Federal range.[113]

"Leaving two guns and a regiment to hold my first position and cover the road leading to Gettysburg, I shifted the remaining portion of my command to form a new line of battle at right angles to my former line," recalled Armstrong.[136, 138] This L position had the shorter leg poised toward Gettysburg paralleling Hanover Road, and consisted of the 1st, 5th and 7th Michigan. While the Long leg on the Low Dutch Road facing Rummel Farm and Cress Ridge, was made up of elements of the 1st, 6th and 7th Regiments.

Stuart sent sharpshooters forward to occupy the barn and out buildings on the Rummel Acres. The Confederates advanced and took up skirmish position behind the Rummel Barn. *"Rummel's barn (was) filled with Confederate sharpshooters, who were picking off the Federal soldiers, they (the Union Artillery)turned their guns on it and drove them out. In the meantime the Federal front line was advanced and drove back that of the Confederates."*[66, 113]

hit it. Gun crews long in practice could knock a door out of a house at a mile distance. Early on gun crews learned to back away and keep their mouths open so as not to blow their ear drums.[134]

Custer called on Pennington, a West Point graduate and nephew of the Ex-Speaker of the House, to silence the Rebel Batteries. In what was undoubtedly the luckiest shot of the war, one of Pennington's 3-inch Ordnance Rifles blew up a Confederate Cannon with a shot right down the muzzle, *"broke both wheels, dismounted the tube"* and rendered it useless. The iron bore 3-inch Ordnance Rifle was by far one of the most superior cannons in the Union arsenal. This light weight counter-

Pennington poses on the extreme right with his 3-inch Ordnance Rifle and gun crew.

Custer instructed Col. Russell Alger to advance the 5th Michigan and hold their ground at all hazards. Fifty men under Major Webber dismounted and started on foot across one and a half miles of open ground toward the opposing forces. Near Rummel's Barn, Confederates charged the 5th who opened up with seven shot Spencers. Alger noted, "*my regiment was armed with the Spencer rifle, being the only regiment on the brigade, and I think in our division, then provided with that weapon.*" The Rebels somewhat confused, hesitated momentarily because of "*That Damn Yankee rifle they load on Sunday and fire all week.*" Stuart had been convinced of an easy victory until intercepted by Custer's Michigan Cavalry Brigade armed with Spencer repeating rifles, "*...their men,*" recounted Armstrong about the 5th, "*behind fences and other defenses as enabled them to successfully repel the repeated advance of a greatly superior force. I attributed their success in a great measure to the fact that this regiment is armed with the Spencer repeating rifle, which in the hands of brave, determined men, like those composing the 5th Michigan Cavalry, is, in my estimation, the most effective fire-arm that our cavalry can adopt.*"[107] Custer himself owned a Spencer Sporting Rifle and would later write the manufacturer: "*I take pleasure in testifying to their superiority over all other weapons. I am firmly of the opinion that fifteen hundred men armed with the Spencer Carbine are more than a match for twenty-five hundred armed with any other firearm*"[58]

The troopers of the 5th continued to provide fire until their barrels grew hot and it appeared they were running low on ammunition.[107] A barrage of gunfire from the rebels' two-banded Enfield muskets burst out and Major Noah Ferry fell fatally wounded. Noting this weak link, the Confederates took full advantage and rushed forward. Webber began pulling the 5th back, all the while pursued by the Confederates. Armstrong at the same time had Pennington open up with Battery M. He then rode in front of the Seventh instructing them to "*keep to your sabres*" and shouted "*Come on you Wolverines.*"

Like a Mad Matador of Madrid, the wind caught the long red tie and it waved in front of the bull-frenzied eyes of the Butternuts in gray as they bellored across the "*corrida ring of battle.*" Taunting them in such a manner it was only left for him to pierce their hearts with the Estoque of his Toledo Blade. That they might lend him their ears? The muleta is swung to the side exposing an obstructing fence. "*Ole' for now the bull will live.*" Running into fences, the 7th could go no further and pulled their revolvers, unloading on the Confederates at point blank range. More Rebels quickly emerged from the woods and began flanking this regiment. Pennington, grasping the situation once again, opened up with his six cannon and began tearing gaps into the Rebel lines. Each time the gaps were closed up. Pennington double shotted the guns with canister and fired as quickly as he could. The 5th fell back and remounted their horses, while the 7th continued to hold the line.

When the Seventh's color sergeant was felled by a pistol shot, Lt. James Birney caught up the pennant empting his revolver into two Confederates who made for the flag and fought off a third lunging with the guidon's spear point before a fourth Rebel struck him with a sabre to the head demanding "*surrender!*"[157] Both were taken, but Birney escaped and returned to the Seventh with the colors that same day.[104]

Armstrong rode Roanoke back to the 1st under Col. Charles H. Town and ordered them forward. Swiftly executing a precision right wheel the 1st came front into line. Several of the horses had thrown their ears back and were admonished and slapped by their riders. One of the horses drew back his lips and reached over to bite the boot of the trooper beside him. Half a dozen horses relieved themselves. A couple more swished their tails, while a few raised theirs to deposit aromatic road apples. The nose flies and horse flies seemed to have found their feast and challenged the efforts of the horsemen to keep their mounts in line. As the 1st Virginia horsemen wheeled their steeds and positioned themselves across the field, the Union horses squealed and blew their taunts in a language only horses communicate in. The Rebel mounts returned the remarks in kind. "*You don't find those Rebel horses handsome do you?*" asked a Michigan boy to his steed.

The Boy General again rode to the front of the First Michigan, Bugler John A. Bigelow, of the 5th Michigan remembered, "*The 1st Michigan is on a gallop. Custer comes tearing along and joins the front, his long, straight saber gleaming in the sunshine. He is bareheaded and glorious. His yellow locks of hair are flying like a battleflag. A brigade of Rebels comes to meet us. Now men, now manhood, now pride, your duty, go! 'Guide center—Charge!'*"[102] The exhilaration of the charge was amplified by Armstrong several horse lengths ahead, imploring them to charge again with the cry, "*Come on you Wolverines.*"[42] It'd started like a drumming cadence, then built to a thundering vibration in their chests as horse hooves were drowned out by the screams and cries of "*...the rebel cavalry, yelling like demons.*" The Rebel yell long renowned in legend disintegrated to the wails and blasphemy bespoken by those damned souls piling onto Charon's boat to be ferried across the river Acheron on their journey to Hell proper.

Confederate Cannon on Cress Ridge, Photo by Roger Hoffman

"Come On You Wolverines," by Don Troiani www.historicalartprints.com

At the cannon roar; explosions of Colt revolvers discharged at point blank range, causing bruises, welts and torn flesh that hung from unsightly open wounds. Each departed soul struggling with dislocated knees, shoulders, stinging hands and ruptured spleens while hearing those ominous words whispered *"Abandon all hope, ye who enter here."*[97] The once heaving sighs of the horses became ear piercing squeals amongst the crashing of equipment, saddles and horse flesh in a collision that *"Like the falling of timber, so sudden and violent that many of the horses were turned end over end and crushed their riders beneath them."* [25]

And then as if an apparition rising from the very fog of battle appeared, the Devil himself, Confederate General Wade Hampton. Mounted on his magnificent 16 1/2 hand bay charger *"Butler"* towering above the fray.[116] Many insisted he was one of the strongest man in the Rebel Army, certainly the most fearless and most dangerous ever to wear Confederate gray. Segregated and momentarily cut off by a squad of Wolverines, he was backed up against a fence where he slashed away with his 1840 wrist breaker, clefting the skull from crown to collar of his first cuirassier.

General Wade Hampton

Pressed harder by the Union combatants who were temporarily distracted by several Mississippi privates who rode in to rescue their illustrious leader only to be struck down by blades of the boys in blue. Suddenly surging across the field of battle came his color sergeant bearing his gold-fringed Southern Cross flag causing Hampton to glance away for a moment and he was likewise subjected to a blow to his head by a sabre wielding Yankee. *"General, they are too many for us,"* besieged the sergeant, *"For God's sake, leap your horse over the fence, I'll die before they have you!"*[140] Blinded by the blood, he took two more blows from the same soldier before he was able to gather Butler's reins and soar over the fence, but not before sustaining a pistol ball in his side.[92, 113, 139]

While the wounded Hampton made good his escape, his color sergeant fell from the saddle, flag falling to the furrowed field, only to be fetched up by a figure in velveteen who lofted it on the tip of his Toledo blade. Bravely waving it before a hail of angry bullets blasted Roanoke's foreleg and brought the Boy General to ground.[19, 116] Battered and bruised, but not beaten it was but a moment before he was back in the saddle of another bay and on his way to battle.[77, 113] By now as much as they tried, it was almost impossible for a horse to cross the field and not step upon a body. Roanoke only slightly wounded, was sent home to Monroe, Michigan where Father Custer helped him to recuperate. Emanuel from then on, only used the horse to haul wood and for a little pleasure riding.[46]

Out numbered 3 to 1 the Michigan Brigade had struck the Confederates with 400 Yankee wielding sabres against an entire Confederate division; a tremendous blow that sent the rebels staggering and retreating. Though it lasted but only forty minutes of severe fighting; it seemed a long day at Rummel's Farm. General George Meade reported the battle as *"indecisive"* but Custer's report of August 22 boasted, *"They advanced to the charge of a vastly superior force with as much order and precision as if going upon parade; and I challenge the annals of warfare to produce a more brilliant or successful charge of cavalry ..."*[137, 138]

The Brigade lost one officer and 28 men killed. Eleven officers and 112 wounded enlisted men along with 67 missing for a total loss of 218 as compared to the Confederate causalities of 181. Of the Brigade's total strength of approximately 1,700 men 481 were killed, wounded or missing. Federals had actively engaged 5,000 men against a Rebel force of 7,000 to 8,000.79 The Michigan Cavalry Brigade had broken the *"Curse of Black Horse Cavalry"* under JEB Stuart and Wade Hampton-thus saving the Union flank atop Cemetery Ridge. On that same afternoon the nearly thirteen thousand Rebel troops in battle lines that stretched over a mile wide advanced from Seminary Ridge in what would become one of the most famous of all Civil War frontal assaults known as *"Pickett's Charge."*

During the holocaust, another classmate of Armstrong's from West Point, would fall on the battlefield. Alonzo H. Cushing, Battery A, 4th United States Artillery defended his guns until the end when Pickett's Charge penetrated his position on Cemetery Ridge. Although wounded for times with a mangled right shoulder, Cushing continued to double and triple shot his guns with canister taking out six-hundred enemy soldiers and almost a hundred horses assaulting his position before succumbing to a shot to the head. A small group of Confederates led by General Lewis Armistead breached the Angle 83 and placed his hand on the barrel of Cushing's hot cannon to help project himself over the wall.[15] Armistead was heard to shout, *"Give them cold steel!"* He would advance no further, himself dying two days later in the nearby George Spangler House, but not before requesting his Masonic watch and personal papers be delivered to his friend and fellow Masonic Brother, Winfield Scott Hancock who desperately wounded, laid but a short distance away. Hancock who had been pleaded by his men to take shelter to the rear had remained mounted during the onslaught commenting, *"There are times when a corps commander's life does not count."* He was struck in the right thigh by pieces of metal and wood from his saddle and although suffering, would survive and lead campaigns in the west after the war Armstrong would serve under him on the frontier.[42,84]

The confrontation at East Cavalry Battlefield, had begun with dismounted skirmishing and ended with violent charges and counter charges that proved to be one of the most ferocious cavalry battles in the annals of American History. Later a captain in the 2nd New York Cavalry was heard to say, *"No soldier who saw him (Custer) on that day…ever questioned his right to wear a star, or all the gold lace he felt inclined to wear."*[109] The contest spanned over three hours and was fought to a draw with Stuart's forces retiring from the field.[133] The humiliation and sting of defeat plagued Stuart for the next year as Union forces lunged and parried through the Piedmont Country of Virginia. *"All I ask of fate,"* wrote Jeb *"is that I may be killed leading a cavalry charge."*

The statement would prove prophetic in May, 1864. Ten Thousand Union horsemen swept into Yellow Tavern on May 11, to oppose Stuart's 3,000. Jeb's thin line was all that separated the Federals from six miles to the southern capital.

Jeb Stuart was shot by Private John A. Huff, Company *"E"* 5th Michigan Cavalry, formerly of Berdan's Sharpshooters and died in Richmond the next day.[142]

In the battle of Gettysburg the fate of the Union trembled in the balance. While the victory was not immediately *"decisive"* its ultimate effect settled the issue in favor of the Union.[53]

With his command devastated and over 6,000 Confederate casualties strewn across the field of battle, Lee spoke to Pickett in quiet tones, *"Your men have done all that men could do; the fault is entirely my own. It's all my fault."*[54]

As the curtains of night closed down on the greatest drama of battle in the history of America, Lee remained astride Traveller, his 16-hand grey American Saddle bred gelding, until well after midnight and rode amongst his commanders reassuring the enlisted men that all would be well. When he finally dismounted, he was too exhausted to stand on his own and was forced to throw his arms around Traveller's neck to hold himself up. Neither he nor *"My Colt"* as he'd called Traveller, moved for several minutes.[131]

Hampton's Duel by Don Troiani. www.historicalartprints.com

VII

"The Pursuit of Lee and Hard Work at Monterey Pass"

Portrait of Rober E. Lee

"When the battle is over, he gayly rides back
To cheer every soul in the night bivouac-
With his jingling spur and his bright sabertasche.
Oh! there you may see him in full glory crown'd
As he sits with his friends on the hardly won ground,
And hear with what feeling toast he will give.
As he drinks to the land where all Irishmen live-
With his jingling spur and his bright sabertasche."[68]

"**W**e must now return to Virginia,"[146] became Lee's objective in the removal of all wounded and supplies from the area in the most efficient means possible. Realizing the consequences and dangers of retreat in an enemy's country, Lee knew he had a monumental task ahead.[147]   No doubt some of his wounded would remain in the enemy's hands and he could only hope they would be treated with a certain degree of compassion.[87] Hoping to simplify his retreat, Lee sent a white flag through the lines proposing an exchange of prisoners.   Meade refused, but would not follow up and initiate an immediate pursuit of the battered and worn Southern Army.   While it had become evident that Meade was victor, he was too exhausted, stunned and war weary to press his advantage and soon became hampered by the torrential rains that had moved in.[100]

A number of officers continued to come forward to encourage him to attack the retreating Confederate army. Pleasonton soon joined the chorus, *"General, I will give you half an hour to show yourself a great general. Order the army to advance, while I take the cavalry and get in Lee's rear, and we will finish the campaign in a week."*

"How do you know Lee will not attack me again?"[144] His timidity was too transparent in his communications with Washington, causing General Halleck to write, *"Push forward, and fight Lee before he can cross the Potomac."*[146] The heavy rains continued for several days bringing the streams, creeks and rivers to flood stage and making the Potomac impossible to ford.[135] *"It is curious to note that, as many soldiers commented, heavy rains almost invariably followed major battles."*[42]

The official U. S. War Department had figured that the Union lost 3,155 KIA;   14,529 wounded; 5,365 captured or missing equaling a total of 23,049 casualties.

While the South suffered 3,903 dead;   18,735 wounded; and another 5,425 captured or missing in action. Their total casualties 28,063. More than the total number of American casualties in the Revolutionary War, War of 1812, and Mexican War combined.[42]

Over 1,000 ambulances were used over the next three days to transport 14,000 Union Casualties. The aftermath of the battle found virtually every church and home in Gettysburg being used as a hospital. The Isaac Lightner house after several days of use as a field hospital had to be abandoned because of the horrible stench. It was never occupied as a home again.[98] *"I found the (Trinity German Reformed) church full..."* Remembered Reuben Ruch, *"...a slaughter house. There must have been 10 (to) 12*

Dead soldier

amputation tables...Doctors had their sleeves rolled up to their shoulders and were covered with blood." Union surgeons worked around the clock for seven days performing amputations. Eva Donner recalled, *"there was so much amputating done there that the seats were covered with blood and they had to bore holes in the floor to let the blood run away."*

Thousands of dead horses littered the fields and streets of Gettysburg after the battle. Artist Edwin Forbes

From Frank Leslie's Illustrated Newspaper, November 7, 1863

75

Emmitsburg vicinity, Pursuit of the Confederate army marching in the rain. Artist Edwin Faorbes

A young Gettysburg attorney William McLean after visiting the McPherson farm remarked about the wounded from both armies lying about with no food or surgical attention. Upon placing buckets of water in his yard for soldiers of the retreating army a Confederate Sergeant admonished his compatriots to not partake as "...*they may have poisoned it.*" Many of the Rebels stopping briefly to loot and remove the clothing from the dead. Bloated bodies of horses, mules and soldiers lined the streets and put off a sickening stench that lasted for days.[72] So bad was the smell that many of those citizens who had remained during the battle were now forced to leave the town seeking refuge in areas of fresher air.[143] Over 72,000 horses were ridden into this battle; between three and five thousand lay putrefying before they were dragged into piles and burned. Those badly wounded were taken to a field near Rock Creek and put out of their misery.[48]

As criticism in Washington mounted Halleck sent a second spurring note to Meade, "*The President is urgent and anxious that your army should move against Lee by forced marches.*" Meade retorted, "*My army is and has been making forced marches.*"[146] Before he would commit to a major move Meade required information on Lee's whereabouts. He felt a reconnaissance-in-force would determine if he needed to send the army west instead of south?[112] Supplies would then need to be moved into Gettysburg, brought north from Westminster. Through the driving rain the cavalry would have to determine Lee's escape route.

Using lessons learned at West Point, Lee adhered to Jomini's Axiom of Article 38: "*A general falling back toward his native land along his line of magazines and supplies may keep his troops together and in good order, and may effect a retreat with more safety than one compelled to subsist his army in cantonments, finding it necessary to occupy an extended position.*" While there are five methods of arranging a retreat, the first being a single mass and the second prescribed dividing into two,[147] Lee chose the latter sending Brigadier General John D. Imboden and two brigades of cavalry to protect his 17-mile-long wounded wagon train, a movement of misery, toward the Cashtown Pass. Lee's second column, also protected by two brigades of cavalry was the supply train of 6,000 wagons, carts and carriages stretching for more than 10 miles long. It traveled the Fairfield/Monterey Pass route, his men herded 5,000 head of cattle; 35,000 sheep, hogs, chickens and turkeys and between 20 to 25,000 horses. The column also consisted of five thousand wounded and broken spirited Union Prisoners of War. The wagons were weighted down with thousands of barrels of flour and other necessities that would feed the Army of Northern Virginia from up to 4 or 5 months. Stuart commanded the remaining two brigades of cavalry that marched by way of Emmitsburg protecting Lee's left flank and cooperating with Ewell's rearguard in holding off the advancing Army of the Potomac.[148] Pleasonton sent Kilpatrick and Custer to ascertain if Lee was going to continue along the Waynesboro-Emmitsburg Turnpike or if he was going to set up a fortified defense on top of the mountain and wait for Meade to attack?

"Our route took us directly across the field of the hot infantry and artillery fighting of the day before," remembered Asa Isham of the Seventh Michigan. *"All will remember the awful spectacle presented."*[104]

Slogging through the rain and mud for hours, the Union Cavalry began to gain on and intercept the wagon train as it ascended South Mountain. At 10 PM the battle began amidst a heavy downpour, *"...the contents of which were spilled all at once,"* remembered James Kidd. *"Such a drenching we had! Even heavy gum coats and horsehide boots were hardly proof against it."*[157] Such a downpour that had little let up since 6:30 PM on the night of the 3rd. Just before midnight on the 4th of July, the Brigade engaged retreating Confederates with their heavily loaded supply train trying to navigate through the Monterey Gap during the heavy rainstorm.[99] Anywhere from 6,000 to 15,000 black teamsters and mule skinners were snapping and cracking whips, while the bellowing , braying and lulling of the animals could be heard for miles. The wagon trains took the lead through the tight mountain pass followed by the Infantry which acted as a strong rear guard. Lee had his cavalry troops set fire to the local barns along the pike which became beacons to guide the rest of his command through the dark.

Confederate Captain George M. Emack was assigned a 20 man detail and 2 mud caked Confederate cannon to hold the Monterey Pass at all hazards. The 1st Michigan took the advance of Kilpatrick's Division slowly picked their way up the winding mountain trail. Armstrong was still riding the chestnut bay he'd mounted when Roanoke sustained his wound at Rummel's Farm. The bay thought to be called *"Lancer"* would be his horse of choice through the next months of campaigning.[149]

When about two miles from the eastern slope of Monterey Pass the 1st came upon a twelve year old girl named Hetty Zeilinger, whom they enlisted to guide them up the mountain in the pouring rain. *"Up this narrow, unknown way ,in a drizzling rain, and enveloped in darkness so deep that the riders, though jostling together, could not see each other, the exhausted, sleepy soldiers on their weary animals slowly toiled, the heavy tread of the horses and the jingling of steel scabbards, the only sound that broke the silence."*[150] The interment drizzle and down pour at times became almost unbearable. *"...the clouds and lightning seemed, and in fact were, below us in the valley,"* reported a correspondent from the New York Times, *"the howling of the storm, and rushing of water down the mountainside, and the roaring of the wind, altogether were certainly enough in that wild spot to test the nerves of the strongest."*[152] The storm and darkness contributed to some of the most confused fighting of the entire war.[153]

"In the midst of pouring rain and intense darkness, save when lightning brought an instant of illumination, the head of the column," recounted Asa Isham, *"...was met by a volley of canister shot from two pieces of artillery posted in the roadway at Monterey Pass directly in front of the summer(Clarmont) hotel."*[104]

Emack opened with his two guns, startling some of the half asleep troopers who in the shock of the sudden cannon bursts tumbled from their saddles. Once order was restored Custer ordered Pennington's guns forward to the center of the road, along with the 6th Michigan who were told to dismount on the right flank. *"We were deployed as skirmishers,"* Captain James H. Kidd of the 6th Michigan recalled.   It was so dark they could see nothing but for, *"Rebels only by the flash of their guns."*[151]

Pennington was instructed to elevate his 3-inch ordnance rifles enough to clear the heads of the dismounted Michiganders who began picking their way up to the summit.

All the while the remaining Confederates continued to blaze away with canister shot from their two cannon, fending off the Union Cavalry for 5 hours. *"My ammunition was entirely exhausted,"* 21 year old Emack exclaimed, *"and some of my men actually fought with rocks; nor did they give an inch..."* In desperation Emack audaciously charged 4,500 Federals with only 8 men, and was wounded five times; shot through both arms and right hand; struck in his right knee from cannon shrapnel and beat about the shoulders arms with sabre blows so severely he was unable to mount his horse. *"At about 3 o'clock AM, finding that he had no force of consequence opposed him, Kilpatrick advanced his cavalry to within my position and gave the order to charge."* [150, 152, 155]

"Our cavalry on the summit," Kidd remembered, was given, *"...The order 'draw sabres...Use sabres alone, (and then told by the colonel) 'I will cut down the first man who fires a shot...Charge.' Away they went."* [151] Over one hundred Confederates rushed to eventually join Emack making only 200 rebels to defend the entire wagon train. Custer ordered Colonel Charles Capehart, who would become the recipient of the Medal of Honor for charging with the 1st West Virginia, to make a mounted assault *"Don't fire a shot just use the sabre."* Capehart along with Custer crossed a bridge spanning over Red Run and with four companies of men captured four hundred wagons and an entire brigade of the enemy. [53]

By 3:30 AM the Union Cavalry had either captured or destroyed over nine miles of Lee's Supply Train taking 1,360 prisoners and countless horses, mules and other livestock destined for Virginia.154 Kilpatrick's losses included five men killed, ten wounded and twenty eight missing. But for all the gain the supply train rolled on eventually crossing into Virginia.152 Still bogged down in mud and bureaucracy Meade would endure and Lincoln lament, *"We had only to stretch forth our hands and they were ours. But nothing I could say or do could make the Army move."* [77]

My dear General,

I do not believe you appreciate the magnitude of the misfortune involved in Lee's escape. He was within our easy grasp, and to have closed upon him would, in connection With our other late successes, have ended the war. As it is, the war will be prolonged indefinitely. If you could not safely attack Lee last Monday, how can you possibly do so south of the river, when you can take with you very few- no more than two-thirds of the force you then had in hand? It would be unreasonable to expect and I do not expect that you can now effect much. Your golden opportunity is gone, and I am distressed immeasurably because of it.

Letter found in Abraham Lincoln's personal papers directed to General Meade. It was never mailed. [145]

*"Dead Soldiers" Illustration found in the National Archives.*w

Of the more than 10,000 land engagements of the Civil War, Gettysburg ranks supreme. In history *"Pickett's Charge"* will be forever remembered as one of the great military maneuvers comparable and memorable to *"The Charge of the Light Brigade."* Although it did not end the war, nor attain an accomplished goal for either the North or South, it remains the greatest battle of the war. It is a reference point, *" the High Water mark of the Confederacy"* and a barometer of every skirmish or conflict that happened before or after that three-day battle. No other battle during the war has brought greater interest,

Union Troops lie flat as Pennington's guns just clear their heads.

"Hidden Soldiers" Harper's Weekly Illustration

controversy or direct study. More ink has been spilled about that battle than the actual bloodshed of the over 50,000 casualties. Probably the single most quoted Presidential speech was inspired by this tragedy and the over 3,000 monuments pay tribute to those heroic souls who suffered, fought and died for those beliefs they held dear. Spiritually and physically exhausted the two armies staggered from the field to regroup and fight on for two more years.[67] But for every American, Gettysburg will epitomize the four years of struggle, when the nation was torn apart and turned upon itself. It tested not only the political and military strengths of the nation, but challenged its economic, industrial and financial resources, straining the psychological and the emotional fabric of all Americans' souls.[81] The four years of war reinvented a style and social acceptance of beauty

and normalcy when thousands of veterans returned home broken, severed and deformed by the scares of war. The reaffirmation of the divided States and the abolishment of slavery changed a course that put the nation on track to a brighter future, but will forever cloud the prism of reflection in how or why we came to that point of provocation to begin with? Who we are today was forged in that caldron of conflict and tempered in spirit and sacrifice that when we emerged from the fire we arrived at a new evolved awareness celebrated in a simple but profound and poignant ideal called, *The United States of America.*"

79

"Red Ties in the Union Army"

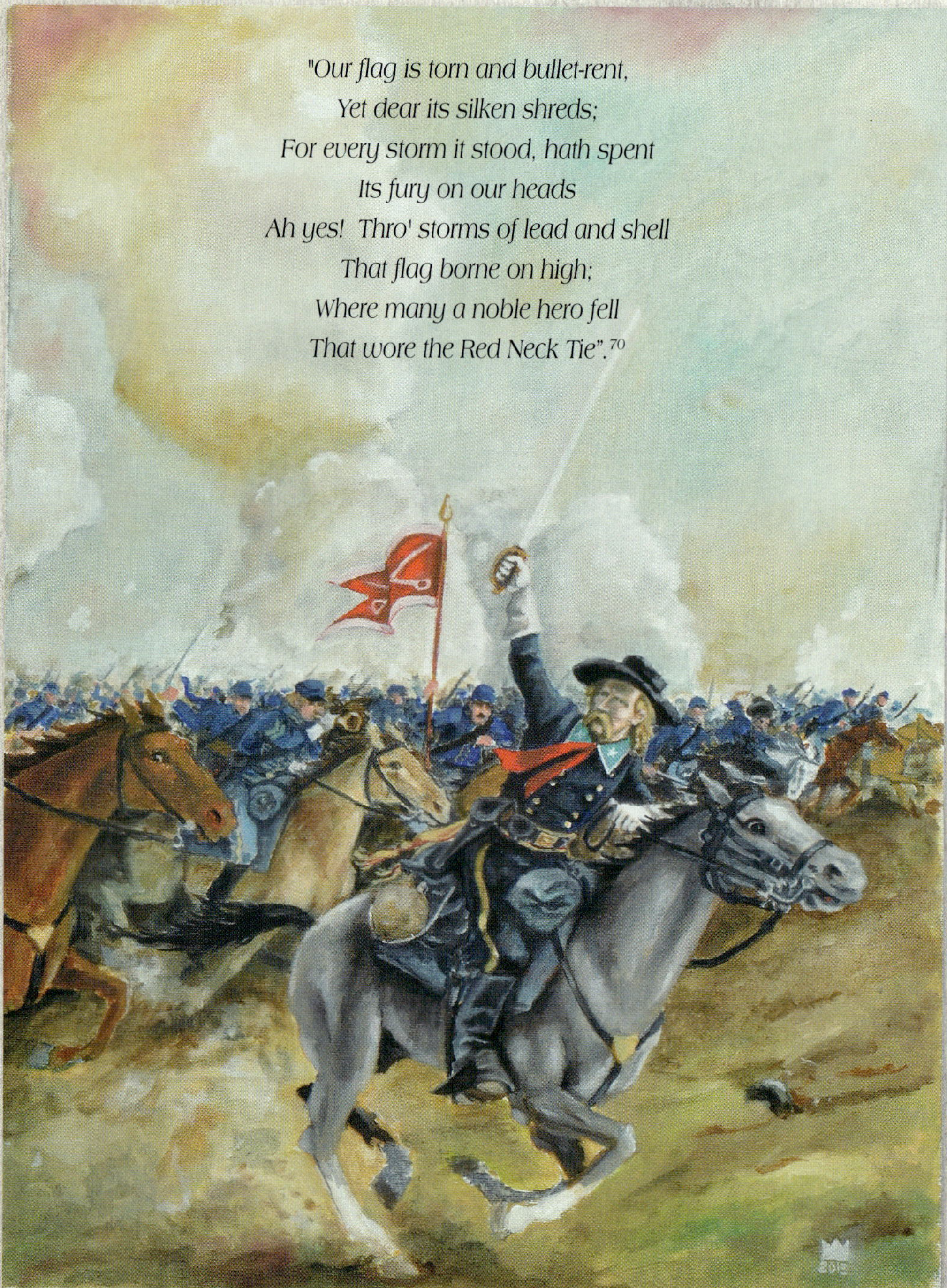

"Our flag is torn and bullet-rent,
Yet dear its silken shreds;
For every storm it stood, hath spent
Its fury on our heads
Ah yes! Thro' storms of lead and shell
That flag borne on high;
Where many a noble hero fell
That wore the Red Neck Tie".[70]

Custer charging at Gettysburg by C. Gómez

By the end of the Gettysburg Campaign which comprised the time between June 3, to July 14, The Brigade had bonded with the Boy General. As they had passed through Trials to Triumphs they had also bonded with one another. But more importantly they had bonded with their horse. Equids156 had carried them and would carry them through battles, long marches and on more than a single occasion, would continue to save their master's life. In all probability that same horse, that man's companion would be there when the next battle would take a comrade's life. Few words could be spoken and the simple lying of a muzzle against his master was all but for the look in the horse's eyes as if to say, *"It will be alright."* A cavalry man understands that the horse is the extension of the man and the man is the extension of the horse. When the two finally became as one; Eohippus had a place to lie his head, a safe haven from the frights of the world-And the man had found a true and faithful friend.

For Custer himself, this story reached back a millennium, back to the dawn of the Horse. It would be a story that would last a little more than a century and a half but would be analyzed, dissected and discussed by over a thousand journalists, historians and students of the Civil War. For better or worse this is a look at George Armstrong Custer's personality and his love of horses. By war's end he had led over sixty successful cavalry charges all of them in front of the advancing troops. He'd lost 11 horses shot from under him (seven alone in the Gettysburg Campaign) and how did this affect him? *I have been through many dangers since last I wrote you. I was in all the battles near Gettysburg and in many cavalry fights before and since...I had three horses shot under me one of which was 'Roanoke' he was shot through the fore leg at Gettysburg by a minie ball(I have the bullet in my possession) and will recover by being taken care of he is improving rapidly now, the other two horses were shot more seriously and I lost both of them."*[19]

"There was one thing about Custer" remembered Captain Ballard, *"he was always at the front, and never still. I believe that he owed his marvelous preservation to that. He never was still, he was always on the move, going just to the identical place where he was least expected."*[62]

Of the dozen or more top Generals of the Civil War, one can hardly forget to mention George Armstrong Custer. He was highly prolific in an age of mass bloodshed and modern warfare, standing out like a relic from the classics of old. A knight errant in manners and decorum riding to the front to bow to his opponents before instructing his bandmaster Major Charles Axtell to strike up *"Yankee Doodle,"* and then in a flash plunge across the field. It was this controversial nature that attracted so much attention. Admired by the public and his superior officers, yet at the same time scorned for his youth and appearance on the battlefield. He designed flamboyant and outrageous uniforms, bedecked with gold and glitter and was deemed, *"a Circus Rider Gone Mad."* The unconventional length of his hair earned him the title of *"The Boy General with the Golden Locks,"* and was emulated by many of his soldiers he led into battle. A flowing red tie he wore around his neck became the trademark of the units he led. Men under him soon adopted the distinguishing badge of honor tearing their own red underwear into cravats and earning the nickname of the *"Red Tie Boys."*

As a token of their fondness, many of his troopers began wearing red ties like the one he always sported after becoming a brigadier. *"The command perfectly idolized Custer,"* wrote a lieutenant of the 6th Michigan Cavalry. *"The old Michigan Brigade adored its Brigadier, and all felt as if he weighed about a ton."* Custer, *" was not afraid to fight like a private soldier... and that he was ever in front and would never ask them to go where he would not lead."*[71]

For pay as low as $13.00 per month, a diet of hard bread, beans, bacon and the recently invented instant coffee, Michigan men marched or rode off, to the constant fear of death from the enemy or infection , into the pages of history.

Their unflinching loyalty and patriotism saw them courting danger in the vanguard of the Union juggernaut. Defeating Stuart's Black Horse Cavalry at Gettysburg was just the beginning. For Custer rank did not dilute his prowess in battle. His men swore by him: Private Victor Comte of the 5th Michigan rode as an escort for Custer during the Battle of Falling Waters remembered, *"I saw him plunge his saber into the belly of a rebel who was trying to kill him. You can guess how bravely soldiers fight for*

Four officers of the 6th Michigan Cavalry, taken in early 1863. The officer seated on the left is believed to be kidd's childhood best friend, Capt. Angelo E. Tower. The seated officer with the mustache is Lt. Charles Bolza, who was killed in action leading a mounted charge at Falling Waters, Maryland, July 14, 1863.

Courtesy John R. Sickles, Merrillville, Indiana.

such a general."[87] And they were willing to follow him into the cannon's breath. And follow him they did, accumulating more causalities than any other cavalry unit during the war. That sacrifice was not without gain. By the close of the war, The Michigan Cavalry Brigade had captured more artillery, battle flags and prisoners than any other Union Command. The Detroit Free Press of October 29th, 1864 reported *"General Custer represents that the victory was the most complete and decisive which has yet been achieved in the Shenandoah. Custer's division pursued the enemy from 3 o'clock in the afternoon until 9 in the evening, driving them into the fields and mountains, capturing whole companies at a time...General Custer's division captured forty-one pieces and several battle flags including the headquarters flag of General Ramseur."*

His adversaries on the battlefield knew him by sight and admired and respected him as a worthy warrior, while a special crack unit of Texas Rangers had but one assignment: *"Kill Custer."* Despite their attempts he came through the War relatively unscathed but for shrapnel wound to his left leg that killed the horse he was riding at Culpepper Court House.

"Their bones are dust, their spurs are rust,

Their souls are with the saints, we trust."[10]

Custer once told an erstwhile comrade, *"the Michigan Brigade...had made his reputation."* And The *Detroit Advertiser and Tribune* October 19, 1864 wrote, *"He has made the Michigan Brigade of Cavalry the pride of the country and the terror of his foes."* They made a perfect pair and for fourteen months The claim to fame was intertwined. *"Custer is the best cavalry general in the world, and I have given him the best brigade to command,"* responded Pleasonton.[69]

In October of 1864 that relationship ended when Custer was transferred to the Third Cavalry Division as a Major General. In November and December he received these letters:

Camps First Brigade 1st Cavalry Division

Middle Military Division-Nov. 18, 1864

But. Major General G. A. Custer,

General

"We, the undersigned officers of the Michigan Cavalry Brigade believing that to some misapprehension is due our disappointment in the long cherished expectation of coming once more under your command, beg leave to reiterate our often expressed wish that you procure our transfer to your division.

"While we would have no act or deed of ours imply the slightest disrespect towards the gallant officer who commands the 1st Cavalry Division we yet wish to convey to you the assurance that on this point the sentiments of the brigade both of officers and men is and will remain unalterable.

"While we are not dissatisfied with our present commander, on the contrary we entertain for him the highest respect and esteem as an officer, a soldier and a gentleman. We yet will be satisfied only with our old well-tried and favorite commander.

"We feel that after two years unvarying success under your command that our destiny is more closely linked with you than any other commander. To forget you or to entertain any other thought than the one that prompts us to ask you to spare no legitimate exertion to bring about this much desired result would be unworthy the 'Michigan Brigade' and would prove misplaced your confidence in us and esteem for us.

"Hoping and believing that with satisfaction to all you will succeed in this as you attempted when with us."

We have the honor to be

Very Respectfully Yours,

Obedient Servants

Members of the Michigan Cavalry Brigade

Headquarters of Mich. Cavalry

Camp Russell, Virginia

December 7, 1864

A second lettler read:

General:

"Having learned that during the temporary absence of this regiment, a paper was gathered up by the officers of the brigade expressive of their strong desire that the 'Michigan Brigade' might be transferred to your division. We have the honor to ask that those of the 'Seventh' may be added to the list, as the sentiments contained in the request, are most cordially endorsed by us. We feel that whatever of admiration or respect we now enjoy at home-or good name and reputation held by the 'Michigan Brigade' in the Army of the United States we owe to you-we therefore cannot but feel the strongest desire that the fortunes of our regiment in the future may be trusted to you who made for us the past so glorious."

We are, General

Your Most Obedient Servants,4

Both letters contained the signatures of Officers and Enlisted men who had served under *"The Boy General."* A further comment was made that if they couldn't get Armstrong to lead them into battle, might they have an old pair of his boots to inspire them? On April 9, 1865 Custer and the Third Cavalry Division formed up to make the last charge of the war. Briefly interrupted by Major Briggs of the Michigan Cavalry Brigade rode up and requested if the boys might have the honor of making that last charge with their old commander?

"If there was any romance or poetry in war," exclaimed Sheridan, *"Custer could develop it."*28 *General Sheridan claimed, "Custer was the only man who never failed me."*

*"Showy, like Murat, fiery like Kearny, yet calm and self reliant like Sheridan, he was the most brilliant and resourceful cavalry officer of his time. Such a man had appeared upon the scene from that day the Michigan Cavalry swore by George Armstrong Custer and would follow him to the death."*5

Custer on horseback was like a centaur, how could men not believe in him? Indeed, for the next decade he would have success as a cavalryman and a leader of men. But it would be for the generations to come that would still

Believe in the Bold.

The Author at Gettysburg from Gettysburg Times July 14, 2012 Photo by Bill Schwartz

Epilogue

On the morning of July 3, 1863, two commanders of cavalry gathered the reins of their horses, each placed a booted foot in the left stirrup of their saddles and swung their right leg over the rumps of their war horses. If the Sisters of Fate so ordained it, the animals would escape devastating injury or grisly death and live to follow their riders' directives throughout the entire engagement. If not, enemy bullets would find their marks in the rider's mount. Unless such a bullet lodges in a vital organ, head, or leg, a horse is often able to withstand five or six shots before crashing to the ground, sometimes pinning a rider beneath him. Adrenaline and shock seem to compassionately kick in and keep the animal on his feet performing necessary tasks until that last fatal injury fells him. An unhorsed rider has little chance of survival himself unless he can quickly find another horse who has lost his own cavalryman. This is but only one perilous possibility a rider of horse faces when he takes his place on line and awaits the command of "*Charge!*"

For commanders like George Armstrong Custer and adversary Wade Hampton, that simple word can seal fate, change fortunes and pronounce a death sentence on man and horse alike. Both men, outstanding equestrians in their own rights, hardly walked before they rode and shared a "*Cavalryman's Dilemma,*" as lovers of horses,

neither man had the luxury of "*saving horses.*" They must and would ride the ones they had, no matter the mortal danger to the life of the horse.

Custer's heart told him not to saddle Roanoke, and Hampton chose well when he tightened the girth on Butler.

In the contest of conscience, Man can be the cruelest living creature on this earth.

And yet, any cavalryman is well aware, a severely injured horse on the verge of death becomes crazed with anguishing pain, sometimes with innards ripped open from gut to cropper, trailing behind the frenzied and fatally wounded animal. "*Herd Instinct*" of the horse will cause it to seek the companionship of others suffering from such cruel agonies, and they will often band together consoling and comforting before the suffering steed succumbs.

To witness a dying horse is one of the cruelest experiences for any human to endure, to helplessly watch and hear the whines of misery. Were it that more humans could view and hear the pains and sufferings their "*deeds*" inflicted on these wonderful animals and even humans less fortunate, then perhaps there would be no need for war. Throughout their history, and sometimes at the expense of excruciating suffering, man's companion and help mate has endured. He asks no questions and only lives to please. The swish of his tail and those four hooves propel a pony across the paddock, straight into our pounding hearts.

My interest in the story of General Custer first came to me through his interest in Hounds and Horses.

I felt if someone cared about animals as this man did, he could not be the hateful individual and image as described by the media and the so- called popular press's accounting of his exploits.

I first met Steve Alexander a decade and a half ago; and although he was wearing a uniform and mounted on horseback, there was something about him that caught my attention.

Beyond the card board caricatures created by Hollywood and emulated by Custer Reenactors, Mr. Alexander had depth.   I saw him numerous times on horseback (and always on a different horse that he had only just climbed upon for the first time the moment I saw him ride!)

Chided as not being a horseman by his detractors, he was able, through his gentle manner and spirit to calm the horse; and despite his unfamiliarity with that certain horse, was able to ride him and ride him well. I'd already heard him describe horses in his first person historical talks, so it wasn't difficult to say yes when he asked me to help him with this work.

The horse as the core and heart of this story was our goal for understanding Custer's relationship with the Horse. Hopefully, the story will allow you to better understand Custer, the Man.

And understanding Mr. Alexander is knowing General Custer.

Jeanne Lyons
Maumee, Ohio
April, 2013

Footnotes

1. *The Bible*, King James Version. *Job 39: 20-24*

2. *Custer and His Times Book Three.* Edited by Gregory J. W. Urwin and Roberta E. Fagan 1987

3. *Addressing the Custer Story*, John Manion, Blaine Beal, W. Donald Horn and Dr. Lawrence A. Frost

GarryOwen Publishers Monroe, MI 1980

4. *Witnesses for the Defense of General George Armstrong Custer*, W. Donald Horn Horn Publications, Short Hills, NJ, 1981

5. *Personal Recollections of a Cavalryman with Custer's Michigan Cavalry Brigade in the Civil War*, James H. Kidd The Sentinel press Ionia, MI 1908

6. *"An Entertaining and Well-produced Primer* Slee Baudrons". Customer Review for Amazon. Co. UK February 4, 2012

7. *The Horse and the Blue Grass Country*, Bradley Smith Doubleday & Co. Inc. Garden City, NY 1960

8. *The New Encyclopedia of the Horse*, Elwyn Hartley, Edwards Dorling Kindersley Publishing, NY, 2000

9. *Top 10 Greatest Military Achievements That Changed the Face of War*, TopTenz.net life, on a short list.

10. *The Book of the Horse*, Samuel Sidney, Bonanza Books, NY, 1985.

11. The *Illustrated Encyclopedia of Horse Breeds*, Susan McBane, Well Fleet Press, NY, 1997.

12. *Glory-Hunter A life of General* Custer, Frederic F. Van de Water, University of Nebraska Press, Lincoln, NB, 1988.

13. *Custer's Ohio Boyhood*, Charles B. Wallace, Harrison Co. Historical Society Cadiz, Ohio 1987.

14. From Conversations with Helen Maxine Dray Gatts, History of New Rumley, as told to the author and E. Leroy Van Horne.

15. *An Unremaining Glory*, Mary Elizabeth Sergeant, Prior King Press, NY, 1997.

16. *Custer: the Life of General George Armstrong Custer*, Jay Monaghan, University of Nebraska Press, Lincoln, NE, 1971.

17. *Ulysses S. Grant, A Novel*, Robert Skimin, Herodias, Inc. NY, 1999.

18. *"Timeline of the Development of the Horse"*, Beverly Davis, *Sino-Platonic Papers 177*, August 2007.

19. Elizabeth B. Custer Collection. CBNM microfilm rolls 1-6.

20. *The Elected Knight*, Henry Wadsworth Longfellow, 1841.

21. *"A review of the human-horse relationship"*, Martine Hausberger, Helene Roche, Severine Henry and Kathalijine Visser, *Applied Animal Behaviour Science 109*. 2008.

22. *"The human-horse relationship: how much do we know?"* I H Robinson, *Equine Veteran Supply*, 1999.

23. *Living with Horses*, Dr. Gala Argent, Eastern Kentucky University Richmond, KY, 2013.

24. *The Human-Animal Bond and Self Psychology: Toward a New Understanding"*, Sue-Ellen Brown, Society & Animals, Koninklijke Brill, NV, Leiden, 2004.

25. *Custer and the Little Big Horn: A Psychobiographical Inquiry*, Charles K. Hofling, Wayne State University Press Detroit, MI, 1981.

26. *Stable Call*, by Rufus F. Zogbaum

27. *"Custer: Hero or Butcher?"*, Robert M. Utley, *American History Illustrated*, February 1971

28. *Civil War Journal: The Leaders,* edited by William C. Davis, Brian C. Pohanka and Don Troiani, Rutledge Hill Press, Nashville, TN 1997

29. *"Cadet Custer Writes Home:* Letters to John Kimmel from G. A. Custer", April 7, 1860. New Rumley Bulletin: Special Edition #2 Tippecanoe Jack, June 5, 1999.

30. *Generals in Bronze,* William B. Styple, Belle Grove Publishing Co., Kearny, NJ 2005.

31. *Introduction to Civil War Cavalry,* E History Archive.

32. *"Custer on the Rise"*, Jeffery D. Wert, *Civil War Times Illustrated Vol. XXXV No. 3,* June 1996.

33. *The Custer Story* Marguerite Merrington, The Devin-Adair Co., NY, 1950.

34. *Hoofbeats in History the Battle of Brandy Station War-Horse Profile of an American Hero,* Nick Nichols, Heartland House Press, Rochelle, VA, 1993.

35. *Cavalry in the American Civil War,* Wikipedia.

36. *"Cavalry Trivia"*, James Acker, Frontier Army of the Dakota, *Post Dispatch, November 2011.*

37. *The Cavalry,The Photographic History of the Civil War,* Francis T. Miller, Castle Books, NY, 1957.

38. *The Custer Companion,* Thom Hatch ,Stackpole Books, PA, 2002.

39. *From the Keynote Address on Sunday, May 21, 1972 at New Rumley, Ohio Paul D. Pfeiffer republished in New Rumely Bulletin Tippecanoe Jack ,June 4, 2005.*

40. *10 Facts About Brandy Station,* www.civilwar.org.

41. *Battle of Brandy Station,* Wikipedia.

42. *Gettysburg Battlefield: the Definitive Illustrated History,* David Eicher, Chronicle Books, San Francisco, CA, 2003.

43. *"Uncivil war pits preservationists against developer"*, Christopher Sullivan, *Jackson Citizen Patriot*, Tuesday March 9, 1993.

44.*The West Point Atlas of American Wars: Volume 1 1689-1900*, Brigadier General Vincent J. Esposito, Henry Holt & Co., NY, 1995.

45. *The Black Knight,* Henry Wadsworth Longfellow, 1839.

46. *General Custer's Thoroughbreds: Racing, Riding, Hunting and Fighting,* Dr. Lawrence A. Frost, J. M. Carroll & Co., NY, 1986.

47. *"Custer's Sabre-An Answer"*, Dr. Lawrence A. Frost, *Research Review Little Big Horn Associates, Vol. VIII No. 3 Fall, 1974.*

48. *The Expendable Horse in the Civil War,* Robert A. Niepert.

49. *"The Civil War Soldier".* Part One: *"Federal Cavalryman" and Part Two: "Confederate Cavalryman"*, Randy Steffen, Patton Museum Society Publication No. 2, Fort Knox, KY, 1962.

50. *"The Horse in the Civil War"*, Deborah Grace, Online Newsletter, July 2000.

51. *Alfred Pleasonton "The Knight of Romance"*, Edward G. Longacre, *Civil War Times Illustrated, Vol. XIII No. 8,* December 1974.

52. *"Aftermyth of War: The Lost Cause is among the casualties in this definitive history"*, Mackubin Thomas Owens, *The Weekly Standard,* Vol. 18 No. 16, December 31, 2012/January 7, 2013.

53. *"Custer, Man of Action"*, Colonel Ralph D. Cole, *Ohio Archaeological and Historical Quarterly,* Vol. XLI No. 4, October 1932.

54. *The Master General: "It's All My Fault"*, Mark Grimsley, *Civil War Times Illustrated*, Volume XXIV No. 7, November 1985.

55. *"The Northern Spencer goes South"*, Wayne Austerman, Volume XXIII No. 3, *Civil War Times Illustrated*, May 1984.

56."*The Spencer: Revolution In Weaponry Goodbye to the Single-shot Musket*", W. Eugene Sloan, *Civil War Times Illustrated*, Volume XXIII No. 3, May 1984.

57. *Weapons of the Civil War*, Ian V. Hogg, Military Press New York, NY, 1987.

58. *"Letter from a Distinguished Cavalry Commander, who has so recently won fresh laurels in the Raid just made under General Sheridan, within the entrenchments of Richmond"*, Eva O. Shillingburg, *Newsletter Little Big Horn Associates*, Vol. VIII No. 8, August 1974.

59. *"Custer's Spencers"*, Col. Philip M. Shockley and LTC. Robert L. Oakley, *Research Review Little Big Horn Associates*, Vol. VII No. 2, Summer, 1973.

60. *Michigan in the War*, J.N.O. Robertson, W. S. George & Co. State Printers and Binders, Lansing, MI, 1882.

61. *"A Cavalry Fight Was On"* Fred L. Schultz, *Civil War Times Illustrated*, Vol. 23, February 1985.

62.*The Chicago Tribune*, Friday July 7, 1876.

63. *The Charge of the Light Brigade*, Alfred Lord Tennyson, December 1854.

64."*Fremantle Tells of Second Day Battle*" from "*The Battle of Gettysburg*" ,W. C. Storrick, *Civil War News*, July 2012.

65. *Pickett's Charge and other Poems*, Fred Emerson Brooks, 1902

66. *"The Custer Image in Confederate Journals"* Part III, John M. Carroll, *Research Review Little Big Horn Associates*, Vol. II No. 2, June 1985.

67. *Gettysburg*, Gettysburg Travel Council, Gettysburg, PA, 1988.

68. *Charles O'Malley, The Irish Dragoon*, Charles Lever, Hurst & Co., NY, 1841.

69. *"Come On, You Wolverines!" Custer's Michigan Cavalry Brigade*, Gregory J. W. Urwin, July-August 1985.

70. *The Red Neck Tie*, Rev. D. Trueman and *The Civil War Memories of Elizabeth Bacon Custer*, Arlene Reynold, University of Texas Press Austin, TX 1994.

71."*Custer and the End of Innocence*", Glenn W. LaFantasie, *The Civil War Monitor*, Vol. 1 No. 2, Winter 2011.

72. *"Eyewitness to War For the horrified residents of Gettysburg, the three-day battle produced scenes of unforgettable Carnage".* James W. Wensyel , *America's Civil War*, Vol 13 No. 3, July 2000.

73. *Important Firearms Auction, The Wiley Sword Collection*, Wiley Sword, Bloomfield, MI, October, 1999

74."*Custer's Civil War Charges*", Don Russell , *The Westerners Brand Book*, Vol. XXV No. 5, Chicago, July 1968.

75. *Michigan Troops in the Battle of Gettysburg*, General L. S. Trowbridge, National Cemetery Rostrum.

76."*The Irish at Gettysburg*", Diana Loski, *The Gettysburg Experience*, Princess Publishing, Inc., Gettysburg, PA, March 2001.

77. *Favor the Bold. Custer: The Civil War Years* ,D. A. Kinsley, Holt, Rinehart and Winston, NY, 1967.

78. *Custer: The Controversial Life of George Armstrong Custer*, Jeffery D. Wert, Simon & Schuster, NY, 1996.

79. *Crazy Horse and Custer: The Parallel Lives of Two American Warriors*, Stephen E. Ambrose, Doubleday & Co. Inc., NY, 1975

80. *Custer: The Life of General George Armstrong Custer*, Jay Monaghan, University of Nebraska Press, NE, 1959.

81. *A Civil War Celebration*, The Carnegie Music Hall, 1998.

82. *Gettysburg National Military Park, Pennsylvania*, United States Department of the Interior, Washington D. C., 1949.

83. *The Illustrated Gettysburg Battlefield Map and Story*, Americana Souvenirs and Gifts TEM, Inc., Gettysburg, PA, 1988.

84. *Masons During the Civil* War, Jon Howey, www.angelfire.com.

85. *A Diary of Battle. The Personal Journals of Colonel Charles S. Wainwright 1861-1865*, Edited by Allan Nevins, Harcourt, Brace & World, Inc., NY, 1962.

86. *The Cavalry Battle that Saved the Union Custer vs. Stuart at Gettysburg*, Paul D. Walker, Pelican Publishing Co., LA, 2002.

87. *Clashes of Cavalry the Civil War Careers of George Armstrong Custer and Jeb Stuart*, Thom Hatch, Stackpole Books, 2001.

88. *The Civil War*, Robert Paul Jordan, Special Publications Division, National Geographic Society, Washington D. C., 1982.

89. *JEB Stuart The Last Cavalier*, Burke Davis, Rinehart & Co., Inc., NY, 1957.

90. *A Popular Life of General George Armstrong Custer*, Frederick Whittaker, Sheldon & Co., NY, 1876.

91. *Man of La Mancha*, Dale Wasserman adapted from the classical novel Don Quijote de la Mancha, Miguel De Cervantes, 1605.

92. *Famous Horses of the Civil War*, Fairfax Downey, Thomas Nelson & Sons, NY, 1960.

93. *Custer or Whoever Heard of Fred Benteen?*, Robert E. Ingham, Helen Harvey, NY, 1977.

94. *.Custer His Promotion in Frederick, Maryland*, Robert A. Servacek, 2002.

95. *Custer Victorious The Civil War Battles of General George Armstrong Custer*, Gregory J. W. Urwin, Associated University Presses, Inc., NJ, 1983.

96. *The Civil War Memories of Elizabeth Bacon Custer*, Arlene Reynolds, University of Texas Press, 1994.

97. *"Inferno"*, Part I, Dante Alighieri's Divine Comedy, Italy, 1322.

98. *Civil War Battlefield Report*, Charles J. Reed, San Francisco, CA, 2005 .

99. *Gettysburg Cavalrymen: 3rd Division, 2nd Brigade Headquarters Staff Army of the Potomac Cavalry Corps Complete and Annotated Roster along with brief description of Marches and Activities during the Gettysburg Campaign June 27- 18, 1863* George A. Rummel III, Bridgeport, WV 2000.

100. *Gettysburg Campaign Chronology*, Steve Schmidt, 2003.

101. *"35 Who Made A Difference: Ed Bearss On the Battlefield, he strikes the mystic Chords of Memory"*, Adam Goodheart, *Smithsonian Magazine Special Anniversary Issue*, Vol 36 No. 8, November 2005.

102. *Custer At Gettysburg* John A. Bigelow The National Tribune May 27, 1886

103. *Under Custer's Command:The Civil War Journal of James Henry Avery*, Karla Jean Husby and Eric J. Wittenberg ,copy of Uncorrected First Page Proofs, Brassey's, Inc., Dulles, VA, 2000.

104. *Seventh Michigan Cavalry of Custer's Wolverine Brigade*, Asa B. Isham, Blue Acorn Press, Huntington, WV, 2000.

105. *Prelude to Gettysburg Encounter at Hanover*, George R. Prowell and the Historical Publication Committee of the Hanover Chamber of Commerce, Burd Street Press, 1963.

106. *Saber and Scapegoat: J. E. B. Stuart and the Gettysburg Controversy*, Mark Nesbitt, Stackpole Books, Mechanicsburg, PA,1994.

107. "Custer's Secret Weapon", Shawna Mazur, *Little Big Horn Associates Newsletter*, Volume XIX No. 6, July 2010.

108. *A Strong and Sudden Onslaught: The Cavalry Action at Hanover, Pennsylvania*, John T. Krepps, Colecraft Industries, PA, 2008.

109. "*Custer: Boy Wonder Under Arms Reality and Myth still collide on the Battlefields of Virginia and Pennsylvania*", Jeffery D. Wert, Civil War Times Vol. XLV No. 2, March/April 2006.

110. *Cavalry On The Roads To Gettysbur: Kilpatrick at Hanover and Hunterstown*, George A. Rummel III, White Mane Books, Shippensburg, PA 2000.

111. "*Custer, Merritt and Farnsworth: The Boy Generals*", Marshall D. Krolick, Civil War, The Magazine of the Civil War Society, Vol. VIII No. 4, Issue XXIV, July-August 1990.

112. "*Gettysburg: The Story of the Great Campaign*", Jeffery Wert, Civil War Times Illustrated, Vol. XXVII No. 4, Summer 1988.

113. *East of Gettysburg Custer vs Stuart*, David F. Riggs, The Old Army Press Ft. Collins, CO, 1970.

114. *The Gettysburg Battlefield Tour Book*, Dr. Michael R. McGough, D. Ed. Thomas Publications Gettysburg, PA, 1991.

115. *Custer And His Wolverines: The Michigan Cavalry Brigade 1861-1865*, Edward G. Longacre, Combined Publishing Conshohocken, PA, 1997.

116. *Protecting the Flank: The Battles for Brinkerhoff's Ridge and East Cavalry Field Battle of Gettysburg, July 2-3, 1863*, Eric J. Wittenberg, Ironclad Publishing Celina, OH, 2002.

117. *Killed In Action*, Gregory A. Coco, Thomas Publications, Gettysburg, PA, 1992.

118. *Join the Cavalry* Sam Sweeney and Troops of J.E.B. Stuart 1861-64, Wikipedia.

119. "*The Stuart-Custer Battle/Hunterstown: The skirmish that changed a battle*", Rick Fulton, *The Gettysburg Companion, Vol. 5 No. 3*, June/July 2008.

120. *Gettysburg*, MacKinlay Kantor, Random House/ Landmark Books, NY, 1952.

121. *Answering The Call to Duty: Saving Custer, Heroism at Gettysburg, POWs and other stories of Michigan's Small Town Soldiers in the Civil War*, Rick Liblong, Arbutus Press Traverse City, MI, 2011.

122. "*Come On, You Wolverines!" Custer At Gettysburg*, Michael Phipps, Farnsworth House Military Impressions, Gettysburg, PA, 1995.

123. *General Custer's Libbie*, Dr. Lawrence A. Frost, Superior Publishing C., Seattle, WA, 1976.

124. *Son Of The Morning Star Custer and the Little Bighorn* Evan S. Connell Perennial Library NY 1985

125. "*Custer earns his star at Hunterstown*", EveningSun. Com, March 2008.

126. *Hunterstown: North Cavalry Field of Gettysburg A Quick Thumb Reference*, Troy D. Harman.

127. *Custer VS Hampton* Troy Harman & Michael Vallone, Pennsylvania Cable Network, July 2, 2005.

128. "*Double Canister At Ten Yards" The Federal Artillery And The Repulse of Pickett's Charge*. David Schultz Rank and File Publications, Redondo Beach, CA, 1995.

129. *Our Most Prominent Ancestor: Norvell Francis Churchill,* Pat Hedgecoth, July, 2007.

130. *Sword That Saved Custer's Life. Prized Possession of HP Family* Royal Oak Tribune, 1959.

131. *"From War Horse to Saddle Horse"* Lynn Weatherman, American Saddlebred, Vol. 16 No. 6, November/December 1998.

132. *"Keep To Your Sabers, Men",* Cowan Brew, *Military Heritage,* January 2011.

133. *"Victory At Last -East Calvary Field" Saturday, July 3rd, 11:00 A. M.* The Battle News Gettysburg, 147th Anniversary, Spring 2010.

134. *"Custer battle brought to life Nationally recognized historian featured during G'burg re-enactment"* Tim Prudente, Special Edition 147th Gettysburg Re-enactment, The Evening Sun, Vol. 147 No. 5, Monday, July 5, 2010.

135. *"One Continuous Fight "Mount Up!" Cavalry Operations During the Gettysburg Campaign",* Eric Wittenberg *Hallowed Ground, Vol. 9 No. 2,* The Civil War Preservation Trust, Summer 2008.

136. *"Cavalry Action Of The Third Day At Gettysburg: A Case Study"* Dr. Lawrence A. Frost, Frost On Custer compiled by Guy Orseno and Tom O'Neil Arrow, Trooper Publishing Brooklyn, NY, 1992.

137. *Creating Enduring Legends: Brigadier General George Armstrong Custer and the Michigan Cavalry Brigade During the Gettysburg Campaign June-July, 1863,* Lawrence Sabbath, 2006.

138. *"No Room For Rebels: The Cavalry Clash at Gettysburg, Pennsylvania, July 3, 1863",* Dr. Lawrence A. Frost, Research Review: *The Journal of the Little Big Horn Associates,* Vol. 4 No. 2 June, 1990 Review: *The Journal of the Little Big Horn Associates,* Vol. 4 No. 2 June, 1990

139. *Peerless Warrior: Wade Hampton III,* Jim McCafferty Blackpowder Annual, Dixie Gun Works, 1991.

140. *Cavalry Clash At Gettysburg,* Roy Morris, Jr. Military History, April 1998.

141. *Lost Triumph Lee's Real Plan At Gettysburg-And Why It Failed,* Tom Carhart, G. P. Putnam's Sons, NY, 2005.

142. *Heroes Of The Civil War,* Harrison Hunt, Military Press NY 1990

143. *The Battle of Gettysburg,* History Learning Site, Ask. Com.

144. *They Met At Gettysburg,* General Edward J. Stackpole, Eagle Books Harrisburg, PA, 1956.

145. *How to Win Friends and Influence People,* Dale Carnegie, Simon and Schuster, 1936.

146. *Gettysburg The Confederate High Tide* Champ Clark Time-Life Books, Inc., Morristown, NJ, 1985

147. *The Art of War,* Antoine-Henri Baron De Jomini, Dover Publications, Inc., Mineola, NY, 2007.

148. *"The Aftermath of Gettysburg: the Story of the Casualties",* Robert D. Hoffsommer, *Civil War Times Illustrated,* Special Gettysburg Edition Vol. 2 No. 4, July 1963.

149. *Traveller and Company: Horses of Gettysburg,* Blake A. Magner, Farnsworth House Military Impressions Gettysburg, PA, 1995.

150. *Retreat from Gettysburg Lee, Logistic, a& the Pennsylvania Campaign,* Kent Masterson Brown, The University of North Carolina Press, 2005.

151. *One of Custer's Wolverines The Civil War Letters of Brevet Brigadier General James H. Kidd, 6th Michigan Cavalry* Eric J. Wittenberg The Kent State University Press Kent, OH 2000

152. *"This Was A Night Never To Be Forgotten" The Midnight Fight In The Monterey Pass, July 4-5, 1863* Eric J. Wittenberg, North & South, Vol. 2 No. 6, August 1999. Wittenberg North & South Vol. 2 No. 6 August 1999

153. *"Ten Days In July. The Pursuit To The Potomac"*, Ted Alexander, *North & South*, Vol. 2 No. 6, August 1999.

154. *The Monterey Pass Battlefield Association*, www.emmitsburg.net.

155. *Monterey Pass (post-Gettysburg) action of 4 July 1863*. First Maryland Cavalry, CSA a Battalion History on Internet.

156. *Horse Power : A history of the horse and the donkey in human societies,* Juliet Clutton-Brock, Natural History Museums Publications, London 1992.

157. *"A General Earns His Star: George A. Custer in the Gettysburg Campaign"*, Kevin E. O'Brien, *Research Review Little Big Horn Associates*, Vol. 11, No. 1, Winter, 1997.

G.A. CUSTER TO THE LITTLE BIG HORN
Steve Alexander

HISTORY • HARD COVER • 176 PAGES
8,2"X11,6" (210 X 297 MM) • OVER 300 PHOTOS

A complete, unbiased, in-depth account of the life of General Custer and his fateful meeting with the Indian tribes at the Battle of the Little Big Horn.

A hard cover, dust-jacketed, lavishly illustrated luxury edition, containing pages full of excitement and unsurpassable knowledge.

Prologue by Dr. Joseph Medicine Crow, last War Chief of the Crow tribe.

THE U.S. CAVALRY, 1865 - 1890
J. Antonio Fernández

HISTORY • SOFT COVER • 52 PAGES
7,4"X10,2" (190 X 260 MM) • OVER 100 PHOTOS

An introduction to the almost mythical United States cavalry between 1865 and 1890, the period of the Indian Wars.

This volume describes the daily life of the men in these cavalry regiments, how they were organized, what their tactics and strategies were and the nature of the enemy they confronted.